Speaking

Is An Audience-Centered Sport

Books by Marjorie Brody

Career MAGIC: A Woman's Guide to Reward &
Recognition

•

Market Your MAGIC: A Guide to Reward &
Recognition

•

Life Without Limits: A Guidebook to Turning Your
Dreams Into Reality

•

Help! Was That a Career Limiting Move?
(coauthored by Pamela J. Holland)

•

Professional Impressions ... Etiquette for Everyone,
Every Day

•

21st Century Pocket Guide to Proper Business
Protocol (ebook only)

•

You Can't Do It Alone: Building Relationships for
Career Success
(coauthored by Amy Glass)

•

"Effective Presentation Skills: Revitalize Your
Speaking Style" (CD-ROM)

**Visit www.BrodyPro.com to purchase any, or all, of
Marjorie's learning tools!**

Speaking

Is An Audience-Centered Sport

Marjorie Brody, CSP, CMC, PCC,
CPAE Speaker Hall of Fame

Career Skills Press

Speaking Is An Audience-Centered Sport

Marjorie Brody, CSP, CMC, PCC,
CPAE Speaker Hall of Fame

Copy Editor: Miryam S. Roddy
Layout: Laura Kremp

Copyright © 2008
Fourth edition
Career Skills Press
Printed in the United States of America

Published by Career Skills Press
815 Greenwood Avenue, Suite 8
Jenkintown, PA 19046
1-800-726-7936
Tel.: 215-886-1688
Fax: 215-886-1699
e-mail: info@BrodyPro.com
www.BrodyPro.com
www.MarjorieBrody.com

Library of Congress Control Number:
2007937148

ISBN:
978-1-931148-17-7

I want to thank everyone who made this fourth edition happen: Miryam S. Roddy for being the driving force; Michele Pepe and Bill Steele for their contributions; Laura Kremp for book layout, and for our "models," Eric Frieman, Dr. Alan Frieman, Pamela J. Holland, Donna Eldridge, John M. Cucinotta, Amy Glass, Bill Steele, Michele Pepe, Ian Shaka Bradshaw, Chris Pepe, Angela Bradshaw, and Regan White.

I'd also like to acknowledge the pros who contributed to this book, BRODY Professional Development staff, and all the clients that I have trained and coached for more than 20 years.

For more information on Marjorie Brody's keynotes,
BRODY Professional Development programs, and
learning resources, write to:
815 Greenwood Avenue, Suite 8, Jenkintown, PA 19046
Visit us online:
www.BrodyPro.com
www.MarjorieBrody.com
Call us: 800-726-7936, 215-886-1688
or fax us: 215-886-1699
You can also e-mail: info@BrodyPro.com

Table of Contents

Acknowledgements

1 Why You Need This Book   1

2 The Preparation Process   4

3 Organizing Your Presentation   20

4 What You Need to Know About Making   46
     & Using Visual Aids

5 The Three Main Parts of Your Presentation   65

6 Practice & Delivery Styles   82

7 Stage Fright & How to Control It   95

8 Delivery Dynamics   105

9 Questions & Answers   144

10 Special Types of Presentations   152

11 Special Occasion Presentations   180

12 Meet the Pros   189

- Effectively Conducting Software and Online Demonstrations -- Michele Pepe
- Ten Tips for Presenting Technical Material to Management Audiences -- William R. Steele
- Presenting Around the World -- Michele Pepe
- When Speechwriters Make the Difference -- Bob Stewart

- Speaking to Lead & Inspire -- William R. Steele
- Why Use Humor in a Presentation? -- Tom Antion
- The Master of Ceremonies -- Ty Boyd, CSP, CPAE
- Voice Training: Who Needs It? -- Ralph E. Hillman, Ph.D.
- Six Principles of Audience-Centered Seating™ -- Paul O. Radde, Ph.D.
- Power, Punch and Pizzazz -- Ray Pelletier, CSP, CPAE
- Selling as a Life Skill -- Tim Connor, CSP
- Presentation Skills for Trainers, Karen Lawson, Ph.D., CSP
- Touching Your Audience's Minds & Hearts with Stories -- Joanna Campbell Slan

Suggested Readings   281
About Marjorie Brody, CSP, CMC, PCC,   284
      CPAE Speaker Hall of Fame
Index   287

Part One

Why You Need This Book

"Each day you get to make a choice whether you are going to take a step forward, remain the same, or take a step back."
– **Kirk McCaskill**, former pitcher, Major League Baseball

During the many years I spent teaching speech and rhetoric at a college, and in the years since as president of BRODY Professional Development, I developed my philosophy that "life is a presentation."

Whether you have chosen a career in business, public service, sales, teaching, medicine, computer technology, or whatever the direction or goals you have, you will be presenting yourself, and your ideas, to others. From going on job interviews to making sales calls, from attending staff meetings to giving full-scale multimedia presentations, your ability to present with confidence and competence will have great impact on your career.

In a fast-changing business environment, you may find yourself interacting with clients or customers thousands of miles from your office doing business through videoconferences or Webcasts. Or, you might find yourself working from home delivering your presentations on the telephone, or via the Internet. Expectations run high in a climate where technology changes as quickly as the seasons of the year.

Business presentations fall into several categories. Speeches are what most people think of when they hear the word presentation. But presentations are much more. They encompass all types of meetings, sales calls, customer service calls, sales pitches to acquire additional business or new clients, and even job interviews. In a large company, there may be hundreds of presentations going on at its various departments and sites. In even the smallest business, there may be two or three: the boss giving a status report before the office opens, a report on a client meeting or results of research. All are presentations.

In our ever-changing business world, the best communicator may be the one who keeps his or her job during a downsizing. The knockout speaker will impress clients and customers far more often than even the best-written report. You need the edge that becoming a polished presenter offers. Whether you will use that edge to become more visible in your company, your community or your industry, is up to you. I offer you the tools to help you achieve your own success.

From the initial steps you must take to organize your

presentation (The Preparation Process), through the collection of data, models of organization, writing your presentation, practicing properly, developing good platform skills, and conquering your stage fright, right up to the final question-and-answer period, everything you need to know to develop your own audience-centered presentations is here for you.

Most people (and books) focus on the speaker, when, in fact, the whole event should be centered on the audience. The speaker could be terrific, but if the particular audience, be it an audience of one or of 1,000, doesn't connect with or get involved with the speaker, the presentation won't work. There is no one style that will work all the time, because there is no one type of audience. There is no right way to speak. Speaking is an art, not a science.

As in professional sports, speakers, like athletes, must be mentally and physically ready to meet their challenges (the audience), they must know their material, and they must know the rules. As you develop your presentations, remember that speaking is an audience-centered sport. Refer to the chapters you need most. And, above all, don't be discouraged if your first presentations are not exactly what you wanted them to be. Even professional speakers have less than perfect performances – but like them, you may be the only one in the room who doesn't think your performance was all it could have been. Keep practicing, and keep presenting so that you will win your game. Good luck.

Part Two
The Preparation Process

"A pitcher should never 'throw' the ball; he should make a pitch.
A pitch has a purpose and a target."
– **Bert Blyleven,** former pitcher, Major League Baseball

Knowing your subject matter (more than just reading PowerPoint), is critical. If you don't know enough about your topic to inform or persuade your audience, you are best off learning it, or not giving the presentation.

Knowing your subject matter is just the beginning, because knowing it is not the same as giving an effective audience-centered presentation. Once you have a level of experience, it is crucial that you take your **PAL**™ into consideration.

Your PAL™ **stands for the three primary presentation considerations: Purpose, Audience, Logistics.** Your PAL™ will be your best friend as you begin the process of learning to become a successful, audience-centered speaker.

Without a thorough analysis of all three, your chances for success will be considerably reduced. You may already know some general information about who your audience is even before you know the topic, but for the preparation process, your first concern will be to establish the purpose of your presentation.

"P" is for purpose

Your presentation will usually fall into one of three types of purposes: to inform, to persuade or to entertain. Before beginning the preparation of your presentation, you must find out or decide which type it will be.

The Informative Speech is given to share information with others. Your material must be interesting enough to capture the audience's attention, and presented in an interesting way to enable listeners to retain as much of it as possible. The amount of information that is retained will decrease as your presentation continues, so that by the end, a great deal of it will not be remembered. However, by reinforcing your key ideas throughout the presentation, by incorporating visual aids, by involving the audience, by using stories and examples, by summarizing your key points at the end, and by the use of well-prepared handouts, much of the information can be retained by your audience. Many of the presentations you will give throughout your career will probably be the informative kind. Giving sales reports, running staff meetings, presenting research, analyzing competitive products, training, even meeting with your boss or staff – all can be informative presentations. Are you involved in volunteer work, church or community service? Chances are you will be giving an informative presentation in your outside activities as well.

Informative speeches are more than just facts and figures. Even a highly technical presentation which must have many facts and figures can be made more interesting to the appropriate audience.

If you have ever listened to a politician trying to get votes, you've listened to a **Persuasive Speech.** A persuasive speech is used to generate action or influence an audience. It can use logic as well as feelings and emotions to appeal to the audience. Successful business speakers also use these tactics to enhance their credibility with the audience. Throughout your life, you will probably find yourself in situations where knowing how to give an effective persuasive presentation will serve you well. Some of these situations may include:

- persuading a prospective client to choose your company
- persuading your employees to work longer hours
- persuading management to fund a project
- persuading your boss to promote you or give you a raise
- persuading voters to vote for you
- persuading a valuable potential employee to join your firm
- persuading your school board to grant funding

You may not give many formal persuasive presentations, but you will certainly find yourself in situations where it is essential to deliver a persuasive presentation in an effective way.

The third type of speech can be **Entertaining.** No, I don't mean stand-up comedy or a motivational seminar. But, you may, at some point in your career or in your personal life, find yourself in situations being asked to give a presentation that falls into this category. This can include everything from a welcome speech to a eulogy. It can be part of a retirement dinner, birthday luncheon, sports banquet, award ceremony or a wedding toast. These presentations are commonplace for some speakers, and rare events for others. When you are asked to give a speech for entertainment purposes, be very clear in establishing what the specific purpose of your speech will be, and who else will be presenting. You don't want to find yourself at a retirement dinner giving almost the same speech as the person who speaks before you. In reality, even your informative and persuasive presentations need to have elements of entertainment – if you want to keep your audience interested and involved.

Now that you have established the type of speech you will be giving, it's time to move on to another crucial pre-speech detail. Who are you going to be speaking to?

The "A" in PAL™ refers to your audience

Who are your audience members, and what are they

expecting to hear? The time it takes you to prepare an audience profile may mean the difference between success and failure for your presentation. If the audience isn't interested in your topic, there is little you can do to make your presentation work. If you are speaking about Medicare reform to college graduates about to face the job market for the first time, your audience will be less than captive. If, on the other hand, you will be speaking to fellow accountants, attorneys or teachers, you already have a great deal of information that will make it easier to create your presentation. If you are speaking within your company or industry, you will probably be able to judge whether or not an audience will be hostile or receptive, depending on the topic. If it's bonuses, you're in luck. If it's downsizing, you may have a difficult time. When you can choose a topic yourself, knowing who comprises the audience will let you select a subject that interests as many members as possible.

The best source for information about your audience will be the program organizer. You can also ask people you know, or get in touch with those who have addressed the same group before. Misjudging your audience, or not knowing who the members are, can have disastrous effects on even the best executed presentation.

Sometimes the program organizer has his or her own agenda. Also, talk to people who will be in the audience. You can check out the Internet, and get annual reports or promotional materials to help you learn more about the group. Read literature about the company and any information pertaining to its corporate culture. Knowing who you are speaking to will help put you in control.

How to develop an audience profile

What do you want to know – and need to know – about your audience members before beginning to create your presentation? Who they are, where they are from, what their positions are (in their industries, companies), and what they might think about your topic are all important. Try to uncover their attitudes toward you and your subject. Who are the decision makers and influencers, and what motivates them? What are their concerns or experiences with the subject you will be talking about? When developing your own audience profile, include the following categories: demographics, psychographics, attitudes, learning styles and identification of the decision makers.

Demographics: What do you know about your audience?

Demographics include audience characteristics such as age, education, occupation, socioeconomic group and marital status, and will affect the way you use language, the information you choose to include, illustrations and examples, and humor if you are including any.

The more details you have about your audience, the

less risk there is of offending anyone and including too much or too little information. You need to know who will be represented in your audience. Will officers of the company be there? Will there be people from many departments with their own agendas, or will you be speaking to a narrower base? Will you be speaking to employees at your own level, or from different levels? The wider the range in your audience, the more difficult it is to tailor your presentation to meet everyone's needs. If you will be speaking in something other than a business situation, it becomes even more difficult to analyze the audience members. Are they all residents of the same town? Do they all attend the same church or synagogue? Are they all the parents of teenagers? Establishing a common bond with your audience members will be easier once you know more about them.

Demographic Audience Profile
When developing an audience profile, include the following demographics:
- Male/female and percentage of each
- Age range
- Income levels
- Race
- Religion
- Introvert/extrovert
- Business/technical
- Education levels
- Where they live
- Where they work
- Marital status

Psychographics: What traits do they share?

Identifying your audience's psychographics is the next step. These traits will help you to further develop your audience profile based upon what you can learn about their feelings and impressions of you and your topic.

Psychographic Audience Profile

A psychographic profile should include the following audience data:

- What do they think about your topic? Is it new to them?
- Have they attended any presentations on similar topics?
- What are their hopes, aspirations, dreams, goals?
- What are their interests?
- Why are they attending the presentation?
- Do they want to be there?
- Are they politically active?
- Have they supported causes like yours before?
- Are they open-minded?

Consider learning styles:

You also want to consider their learning and behavioral styles. By understanding these styles (visual, auditory and kinetic), you will be able to decide the best way to present your information.

Identify decision makers (and the influencers!)

Is the company president going to be there, your immediate supervisor, or someone you are trying to influence? Knowing in advance if decision makers will be in the audience will help you target your remarks. It will also let you know who the audience will be looking to for feedback and impressions. Capturing a positive reaction from decision makers in attendance can make your presentation a success even if others in the audience disagree. If you have identified a decision maker in the audience, avoid a common pitfall – addressing your comments to this person or looking primarily at him or her during the presentation. This could backfire by making the rest of the audience feel less important. Take into account the people who influence the decision makers. Their opinions count.

WIIFM: What's in it for me?

Each member of your audience comes to a presentation with an agenda of his or her own, and wants something from you, the speaker.

What these audience members will be looking for may be revealed with answers to the following questions:

- What have their experiences (with the topic) been?
- Why are they there? Do they want to be/have to be?
- What do they hope to get out of the presentation?
- What are their important issues?
- Are they there with an open mind?
- What do they expect from you?

"L" is for logistics

Why are logistics important? Have you ever had a long lunch immediately followed by a slide presentation in a darkened room? That's a sure combination for an audience dozing, if not outright sleeping. A well-prepared speaker takes time in advance to find out details that can ease tension on the actual speech day. For example, if the speaker at the presentation following that long lunch kept the room bright, used more interactive visual aids, and kept the topic moving quickly, the chance of having post-lunch nappers would have been greatly reduced, if not eliminated.

When determining logistics, find out the following:
- How many people are in the audience?
- What time will you be presenting?
- Who speaks before you? After you?
- How much time will each speaker have?
- How much time do you have?
- What happens if speakers run over their allotted time limits?
- How long will there be for questions and answers?
- Will the Q & A be held at the end of each speaker's portion, or will they be at the very end?
- Where will you be presenting? What is the size of the room and how will it be set up?
- What equipment is available? Will a microphone be provided or must you bring your own?
- How is the room arranged?
- What is the exact location of the presentation, its correct address, room, floor and directions to the site?

You will also need to know how many people will be in the audience, so that you have the appropriate number of handouts and use the correct visuals for that size group.

When you get to the site, find out where the restrooms are so you won't be wandering around looking for them during the program breaks.

Collecting & using your information

Collecting information to support your ideas will take the most time in the preparation process. Once your PAL™ has been clearly defined, you already have your first step completed. Now you will write your central theme – one sentence which defines your objective.

What do you want your audience to know, do or feel as a result of your presentation? Use a verb – to inform about, to get commitment for, etc. The theme is what you want to achieve as a result of the presentation. It must be clearly defined and doable. Once the central theme is written, your next step is to collect information. Since you are the expert, start to gather information by using what you already know. Brainstorm and write down key words and phrases about your subject. I use a large wall filled with different-colored self-adhesive note squares to create my speeches. This allows me to move information around as I am outlining my presentation.

After outlining what you do know about the topic, move on to using outside data and research. All information should be current, relevant, and correct. Using other people's theories and presenting them as facts can get you in trouble and cause your audience to question your credibility.

Facts and statistics alone often become data dumps, not the most interesting or memorable way to give information. You can use facts and statistics to support and validate your own ideas. For example, if you are speaking about the value of hiring consultants instead of full-time employees, you can use researched evidence to back up your claims showing reduced costs of employee benefits, lack of paid vacations, and other company cost savings. If you are trying to convince a group to take action, use statistics to illustrate what previously happened to those who took (or didn't take) a similar action. For example, if you are trying to get your neighbors to support a community watch program, show statistics which demonstrate the reduction in crime for city blocks with community patrolling vs. streets without patrols.

Using examples and stories can help reinforce the points you want to make to your audience. Relating personal anecdotes is not only entertaining, but allows your audience to visualize a situation where something happened. For example, if your topic is stricter controls in airline baggage handling, you might use your own trials and tribulations as a business traveler waiting for checked sample cases only to receive them opened and with missing items.

Visualizations are also helpful. To illustrate misleading packaging, you might show two cans of tuna, both exactly the same size, but with differing weights. By reading the labels and showing the cans to the audience, they will be able to see as well as hear your point. And it also makes your presentation more memorable.

What types of outside data work best? Using information other than what you know should enhance and add color to your presentation. If you are preparing a persuasive presentation, now is the time to bring in the experts to support your theories. Who else thinks like you do and has credibility? Has a nationally recognized expert been quoted saying something to support your ideas? Have respected journals published statistics to back you up? If you can demonstrate to audience members the logic of your position, and back it up with the opinions of experts, it will help them to better understand your position.

You can use outside data within your presentation in various ways. Examples, stories, quotations, comparisons and contrasts, statistics and visual aids can all make your presentation come to life for the audience. Which ones to use will depend on your topic. For example:

- Using examples can illustrate your point but not validate it. Use facts and figures for validation.

- Quotations give you the chance to add an expert's opinion to back up your own, or they can be used as attention-getters.
- Comparisons provide similarities, contrasts provide differences. Use them to help audience members relate what they already know to what you want them to know.
- Statistics are useful to support your own theories or disprove others.
- Visual aids help audiences to understand your information, visualize places or things they might not know of, and can be used to bring statistics to life.
- Stories add entertainment for the audience. Share your stories but keep them relevant to the topic and not overly long.
- Appropriate humor can add a light touch, and laughing is a proven way to relax an audience.

While humor can be incorporated into your presentation, it's important to remember some guidelines when using humorous examples and anecdotes.

Some guidelines to consider before using humor:

- If humor does not come naturally to you, don't use it until you are comfortable doing so. Practice at least three to six times, and if it still doesn't come out comfortably, leave it out of your presentation.
- If you are not comfortable with long stories, use one-liners.
- If you're not sure about a joke, try it out on a friend, spouse, or co-worker. If in doubt, leave it out.
- Try to surprise your audience with your humor; don't

start off by saying, "I want to share this funny story with you." It's better to surprise them with it.

- If no one laughs, try to say something to ease the silence, for example: "That's the last time I ask my attorney if something is funny." If the humor makes a point, remember, it's OK if they don't laugh.
- Don't laugh too hard at your own jokes. It's OK to let your enthusiasm for the anecdote show, but laughing too hard is in poor taste.

If you choose to use humor:

You can use humor successfully if you stick to the guidelines. First, make sure it's appropriate for the occasion. Unless it specifically pertains to your company, you're sure everyone there will understand it, and no one will be offended, proceed with caution. Inside company jokes can be very funny. But only if everyone gets the joke. When used properly, humor can be a wonderful icebreaker. In a room where few know each other, it can make friends out of strangers and sympathetic listeners out of apathetic ones. Stories about yourself are safest; everyone enjoys a good joke at someone else's expense – when it's done with good taste and the joke is told by you, about you.

If you have decided to use humor, here are six guidelines:

1. **Remember the punch line.** A great story isn't so great if you can't remember the end. It will also lose credibility for you with the audience.
2. **The anecdote should relate to your speech and be**

appropriate. Don't speak about your children's exploits when the group includes infertile couples.

3. Have good timing. Practice your anecdote. Tell it to several people and watch their reactions. If the story doesn't go over well, modify or eliminate it. Practice until you feel comfortable with the material.

4. Don't be cruel. You might think fat jokes are funny, but someone in the audience may have had a weight problem or is sympathetic to someone who does.

5. Don't use vulgar language. Even if your audience is a room full of "the guys," it's never appropriate.

6. Humor doesn't always travel and it might not work overseas. This is even true regionally within the United States. Always keep your audience in mind. What's funny in New York may not be funny in Memphis.

Remembering humorous anecdotes may seem easy when you first hear or think of them, but chances are, like anything else, you'll forget the story if you wait to write it down. Save yourself some grief and write the story down as soon as you think of it or hear it.

Part Three

Organizing Your Presentation

"The most important thing is how a guy prepares himself to do battle."
-- **Hank Aaron,** Hall of Fame baseball player & legend

Unlike a paper which people can read at their own pace, and re-read when necessary, you have only one chance to be clear in an oral presentation. The method of organization that you choose will be a reflection of the type of speech you will be giving: informative, persuasive, or entertaining. Your audience members will depend on you to show them the way to understanding; a well-organized presentation acts as a road map to guide the audience from one point to the next. It should have a well-designed introduction, a body that leads them where you want them to go, and a strong conclusion to tie it all together.

The rule of thumb suggests that you cluster your ideas into three main points. The reason behind this is that it is easy to remember. All context must reinforce your central theme. Obviously, there are times that you will have more or less than three, however, by all means avoid a laundry list of items, if you want the audience to follow what you are saying and to retain the information. Although you have a great deal of excellent material, take into account the amount of time that is available (the "L" in PAL™).

Once you have gathered your material and begin to organize it, think in terms of "must know," "should know," "could know." If there is time, include it all. If time is limited, or cut off at the last minute, you will immediately know what you can eliminate without sacrificing the key information.

Developing Your Outline

Develop an outline as a planning tool to give shape and form to your presentation. Regardless of the purpose of your presentation, the outline will help you to create an effective presentation. The preferred method of outlining is the **phrase outline method.** Phrases are long enough to remind you of what you want to say, and short enough so your attention will be on the audience and not on the outline. Most points will be written as phrases or bulleted items. The problem with writing full sentences is that speakers have the tendency to read. Anything that is written should be for the ear, not the eye. Keep the language conversational. You will need transitions to prevent gaps between you and your listeners. Transition sentences are used between the review of your main points and your final, memorable statement. Transitions, numbers you need to remember, or other important statements that must be spoken accurately, can be written out. Transitions enable the speaker to repeat ideas without being redundant. They help move the listener from point to point, and, should they be drifting, transitions reiterate what has just been said. Examples of transitions are: "another way to look at," "along with," "we have just covered," "let's move on to the next point" and "the second point is."

Organization of the Informative Speech

The informative speech can effectively be organized in one of six ways:

1. Chronological order. Arranged in order of occurrence or a time sequence. If your topic follows in a progression, you might use a time line to illustrate the process. Visual aids can be effective in demonstrating the time span to your audience.

Chronological Order
50 Years of Change in Television Viewing Behavior*

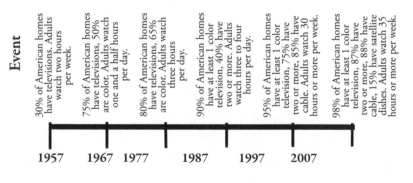

Event

| 30% of American homes have televisions. Adults watch two hours per week. | 75% of American homes have televisions, 50% are color. Adults watch one and a half hours per day. | 80% of American homes have televisions, 65% are color. Adults watch three hours per day. | 90% of American homes have at least 1 color television, 40% have two or more. Adults watch three to four hours per day. | 95% of American homes have at least 1 color television, 75% have two or more, 85% have cable. Adults watch 30 hours or more per week. | 98% of American homes have at least 1 color television, 87% have two or more, 88% have satellite dishes. Adults watch 35 hours or more per week. |

| 1957 | 1967 | 1977 | 1987 | 1997 | 2007 |

*Hypothetical example

Chronological is a good model for defining work projects: Where we were, where we are, and where are we going.

2. Spatial order. Since spatially organized presentations pertain to the nature of space, they are most effective when combined with visual aids. If your presentation was about the differences in movie theaters' treatment of patrons in wheelchairs, visuals showing the different layouts of the theaters would help the audience to visualize the best (and worst) ways to arrange the seating for these patrons.

<u>**Spatial Order**</u>
<u>**Setting Up Classroom Learning Centers**</u>

<u>Classroom A</u>	<u>Classroom B</u>	<u>Classroom C</u>

3. Geographical order. This presentation is also arranged spatially, but by geographical space. If you are discussing the early colonization of the United States, using visuals of how the states looked in relation to each other during different periods in U.S. history would effectively demonstrate to the audience the different geographical areas involved, their sizes in relation to each other, and changes compared to recent history.

4. Topical order. This type of speech takes a large topic and subdivides it. Think of the topic of private public schooling today. Private schools could be further divided by parochial, same sex schools, boarding schools, and day schools. Public schools could be broken down by inner city vs. suburban and rural. This method works well for discussing a variety of products.

5. Past – Present – Future. This method of organizing works well for describing projects. It gives context as to where we were, where we are, and where we are going.

6. Cause and effect. The presentation organized by cause and effect has a distinct order. First, what has happened, or what will happen, and then what the results will be. For example, if your company allows job sharing for some employees but not others, you may have disgruntled employees, possibly risk lawsuits, and end with an unproductive work force. You also can give multiple scenarios and conclusions using the cause-and-effect format.

Informative Presentation Planning Sheet

To download a copy of this worksheet, go to
http://www.brodypro.com/support/plan_pad.html

Informative   Planning Worksheet

Central Theme:

Consider: Purpose, Audience, and Logistics (PAL™)

Main Point:

Supporting Data:

Main Point:

Supporting Data:

Main Point:

Supporting Data:

Transition →

Transition →

INTRODUCTION 10 - 15%

Grabber:

WIIFT:

Source Credibility:

Preview:

CONCLUSION 5 - 10%

Review:

Memorable Statement:

Creating Persuasive Presentations

Have you ever ordered anything while watching a TV commercial or infomercial? Did you ever buy a magazine subscription over the telephone or from someone who came to your door? If you answered in the affirmative, then you have responded to a persuasive presentation. How can you be persuasive? By using various methods of proof to convince your audience members to do or think what you want them to. The ancient Greek philosopher Aristotle talked about using **Logos, Pathos and Ethos** as methods of persuasion, and they are just as valid today.

Logos in Greek means reason, and is how the word logic is derived. It contains your facts and figures, statistics and other forms of documentation. This type of information can be slanted to support the presenter's own philosophy. Just listen to any politician at election time. With the same campaign issues, one politician will try to convince you that the only way to improve things is to raise taxes. His or her opponent will try to persuade you that the only way to improve things is to lower taxes. Now the lower tax position may be the one most people will go for right up front, but a successful politician can persuade voters that increased taxes is a good thing! Logos also includes a logical progression of ideas. Logic hits the head.

Pathos, also from the Greek, refers to using emotions. This is the method for appealing to the needs, wants, and desires of your audience members – in other words, emotion hits the heart and gut. Most decisions are made using a combination of logic and emotion (logos and pathos). Understanding the needs of your audience members is vital to persuading them. You want them to feel good about their decisions, and can combine logos and pathos to do this. While many scientific thinkers claim to use only logic to make decisions, we are more subtly influenced by emotion than we may care to admit.

Ethos is the third mode of proof. It is the speaker's credibility. How are you perceived by your audience? This can be determined by your education, degrees, age, gender, political affiliation, reputation and position in your company. If people trust you, they will be more likely to believe what you are saying or do what you recommend. Since your audience members filter the information they hear based on their perceptions, your ethos is critical.

Establishing credibility

What are the major components of credibility? Credibility consists of three components: perceived trustworthiness, perceived competence, and perceived conviction. Regardless of whether or not the presenter is actually any of these things, the audience's perception is what matters. If the audience perceives the presenter as being trustworthy, competent, and having the power of his or her convictions, that is what is important. It is then up to the speaker to confirm what the audience believes. If, however, credibility is an issue, how do you deal with it? Your competency can be established by an introduction that states your credentials and accomplishments. The force of your convictions will be established during your presentation as you demonstrate your knowledge and display your convictions.

Your trustworthiness however, is more difficult to establish. A classic approach to establishing trust is through common ground. It involves sharing the similarities between you and your audience -- demographics, attitudes, and experiences all count toward establishing trust. For example: "I've lived in Philadelphia for the past 25 years, as have many of you. I am a product of Philadelphia public schools, as are many of you. I've been paying Philadelphia city taxes for the past 25 years, as have many of you. I want to pay less, as do many of you." You have established common ground – where you live, where you went to school, taxes, dissatisfaction with the taxes you pay. All these common bonds count toward establishing trust.

Purpose

Most successful presentations have some elements of all three modes of persuasion. The speaker's style and analysis of the audience and topic help him or her decide how much of each to use. In addition to having three possible modes of persuasion, persuasive presentations also have three levels of persuasion: to motivate, to convince, and to call to action.

Motivation is the first level of persuasion. You want to excite members of your audience about what is being shared with them, but you probably won't be altering their opinions or beliefs. Motivation can be as familiar as a church sermon, or a speech by the coach of a sports team getting his players fired up before their game. You want your audience members to feel good about what you are telling them and about themselves. All presentations should be motivational.

The second level of persuasion is to **convince.** You want your audience to change its opinions or to develop the same opinion as yours. You may not want them to do anything but change their minds. If they haven't yet formed an opinion, you want them to adopt yours. For example, if your company does not offer on-site day care, and you believe it will benefit both employees and the employers if they open a day-care facility, you want your audience to share your opinions.

Then you move on to the third level of persuasion, a **call to action**. You want the audience to do something, in the case of day care, to join with you to convince management that on-site day care is essential for the company to provide. This is the most difficult level of persuasion to achieve. Any persuasive presentation can be prepared using the same method. Developing an outline will be the first step. Following the format provided here, first state your ultimate purpose: motivate, convince, or call to action. Be clear about your objective.

Audience

Next, identify your audience and the attitudes you will be facing: favorable, hostile, apathetic, uninformed, or a combination – favorable mix or hostile mix. In order for your presentation to be effective, you need to have an understanding of who you will be speaking to, and, hopefully, something about their mindset. When determining this attitude, keep the following six audience types in mind:

Favorable: They already share your opinions and probably want what you want. For example: other employees who are currently paying for off-site day care and who are stressed both paying for it and keeping work hours that match the day care's hours. It's rare to get an entirely favorable audience.

Hostile: First, understand why the audience is hostile, and exactly what the hostility is towards. Are there issues: time, expense, philosophy, you, etc.? For example: I once traveled across the country to give a seminar on business etiquette in a corporate setting to middle managers in a large corporation. When I entered the meeting room and went to introduce myself, no one greeted me. I wanted to diffuse the situation right away, so instead of opening the session by talking about what I hoped to cover in the seminar, I began by asking them why they objected to the topic, and why they thought it was a waste of time.

Now the participants knew I would be listening to them, and they began to open up and talk about their feelings and why they felt hostile. One of the things they objected to was why upper management thought they needed etiquette training, and wasn't it common sense anyway? When I explained that upper management had already taken this same program, and that there was much more to business etiquette than common sense, they began to respond to me in a positive way. They knew that I was listening to them and dealing with their objections. On another occasion, I was asked to facilitate a program that was being rolled out to a sales department who thought it was a waste of time. Their feelings were obviously negative, so I opened by asking why they were against the program. After listening to why they didn't think they needed the training, I was able to turn things around by telling the department about improvements that came from the program. I then was able to ask them about areas where they could improve their skills, and they began to see that I was interested in helping them. I demonstrated that I understood their concerns and was there to work with them.

Apathetic: They really don't care about what you have to say, and must be made to realize how they will benefit before responding favorably. For example, people in your company without young children probably won't care whether or not there is on-site day care, but by using examples of how they will benefit from it (i.e.: less time for co-workers to be late, absent, or have to leave early to meet day-care schedules), on-site day care is a worthwhile project for them to support.

Uninformed: They are not opposed to what you have to say, they just don't know anything about it. Your job is to educate them. For example, if you want me to support on-site day care, you have to demonstrate the benefits for me and for the company. Maybe as a supervisor, I won't have to cover for employees who are late or absent because of child care problems – and asking workers to stay late will be easier when they know they can see their children and even have meals with them before returning to work. The company benefits and the supervisors and employees benefit.

Mixed: There are **two types of mixed audiences:** the *favorable mix* and the *hostile mix.* The favorable mix includes favorable, uninformed, and apathetic members. You will have to inform the uniformed and convince the apathetic that there is a real need or benefit. If there is even one hostile member of the audience, the entire audience can shift and align themselves with the hostile member, and, if so, this group is identified as a hostile mix. Your audience analysis should have prepared you for the hostile mix, and your challenge is to disarm the hostile members and win them over as soon as possible. Sometimes the real audience isn't even in the room. The ultimate decision-makers may be hostile, and the group at hand will need to persuade them.

If you are prepared for a hostile audience, you will be ready for any mixed group. The hostile mix is probably the most difficult audience to work with. Organize your presentation to bring up comments like, "If we go with on-site day care, what are the benefits to your department?" If hostile mix audience members believe that you are receptive to their concerns and not afraid to talk about them, they will be more apt to listen to your points later on. It is up to you to determine and address the reasons for hostility. It probably has nothing to do with you personally. There may be budget cuts, unfair promotions, or other grievances that have nothing to do with what you want to talk about. A good listener will gain the respect of the audience. If you are presenting information that you know will be received negatively, bury the negatives in the middle of your presentation and end with the positives. Don't be evasive, you will be found out sooner or later.

Logistics

After determining your purpose and audience, think about the logistics of your presentation. How long will you have to present? What time of day? Are you part of a group? If you are part of a team presentation, what is the order? How large is the audience? What types of visuals will work best?

Then, collect your information. Make sure this information is pertinent, current, accurate, relevant, and appropriate. For example, if you will be speaking about on-site day care in your company, make sure you have the facts and can support them with evidence. If you are appealing to your audience members for support, and sense hostility because they don't have any children or perhaps their children are already out of school, you will have to find the "hot buttons" and appeal to them on that level. Perhaps you have research that proves on-site day care improves the productivity of employees who use the service and other employees as well by helping to alleviate tension in their departments. You will be able to relate this information, meet the audience needs, and keep your own agenda at the same time. When you are preparing your data, keep the audience and its needs in mind at all times.

Organizing The Persuasive Presentation

A persuasive presentation can be organized using one of three methods: proposition to proof, reflective, or motivated sequence.

Proposition to Proof. In this method, your proposition is stated at the beginning of your presentation. Your audience members know right up front what you want from them. Then, you prove your proposition using three to five points of evidence and emotional appeal, and transitions that connect the ideas. Finally, you review the evidence and end with a strong closing statement. Since you want your audience members to be receptive to what you are going to say, you don't want to offend them in the beginning of your presentation.

To make people want to change their point of view, give them new information presented in a way they will be able to easily understand. This method works well with favorable audiences, and is possible with some work for uninformed, apathetic and favorable mixed groups, but is not a good choice for a hostile or hostile-mix audience.

Example of a proposition to proof situation:

Proposition: "I recommend our corporation fund and operate an on-site day-care facility."

Proof:
1. With their children on-site, employees won't feel stressed by rushing to get to work on time or having to leave early to pick up children.

    Transition: Not only will this reduce stress, but it will create loyalty.

2. Since on-site day care can be either fully or partially funded by the corporation, this is a strong incentive for employees to stay with the corporation.

    Transition: Another benefit of a daycare is less absenteeism.

3. Other corporations with on-site day care have reported only favorable results and cost savings due to less employee absenteeism.

Call to Action: "Let's meet next Thursday so we can make a decision. I urge all of you to see the benefits for both the company and its employees."

Persuasive Presentation Planning Sheet
Proposition to Proof

Persuasive *Proposition to Proof*

Central Theme:

Consider: Purpose, Audience, and Logistics (PAL™)

Proposition:

Proof & Supporting Data:

Proof & Supporting Data:

Proof & Supporting Data:

Transition

Transition

INTRODUCTION 10 - 15%

Grabber:

Source Credibility:

WIIFT:

Preview (optional):

CONCLUSION 5 - 10%

Review:

Memorable statement:

Motivated Sequence (Problem to Solution). This is the method *used the most in sales.* You lead audience members to the brink of action, and then provide them with the means to act. The motivated sequence either identifies a need in audience members, or makes them aware of a need. You really are building a case that a problem exists. You then supply the means to satisfy that need, or solve the problem. It is up to you to make the solution appealing to your audience. Any negatives to your plan should be included in the middle of the presentation.

Example of motivated sequence:

<u>Problem</u>

Get attention: Are you holding yourself back in your career because of an inability to present and sell your ideas?
Create need: In order to become an effective salesperson, you must be an effective presenter. Studies show ...

<u>Solution</u>

Satisfaction: If you take a BRODY seminar, you will learn how to:

- Organize your ideas
- Read your audience
- Control your stage fright
- Move and use visual aids
- Handle questions comfortably

Visualization: With these skills, you will be able to connect with your audience and sell your ideas. Picture yourself as a regional sales manager ... .

Call to action: Telephone, fax, e-mail, or visit our
Web site at: www.BrodyPro.com

Knowing how to present persuasively is critical to career
development, and also will benefit you in other areas of your
life. The ability to influence others' beliefs and motivate
change is a powerful tool to be used carefully and selectively.

Persuasive Presentation Planning Sheet
Motivated Sequence

Persuasive **Motivated Sequence**

Central Theme:

Consider: Purpose, Audience, and Logistics (PAL™)

Problem or need:

Solution or Satisfaction (features/benefits):

Visualization:

Transition

INTRODUCTION 10 - 15%

Grabber:

Source Credibility:

WIIFT:

Preview (optional):

CONCLUSION 5 - 10%

Review:

Appeal to action:

Reflective. Using this method, the problem is stated and proven in the beginning of the presentation. This works most effectively if the speaker and audience then agree on a criteria to evaluate each of the possible solutions and to ultimately make a decision. After the problem and the criteria are agreed upon, the solutions are offered and evaluated against the criteria. Effective speakers often present the positive points of each solution, then smash them with evidence to the contrary using the agreed upon criteria as a basis of evaluation, and finally present the best solution supporting it with plenty of evidence. The solution you like can mention the negatives first and then build up the positives against the criteria. If you are not strong when presenting your beliefs, you will not be able to convince others that your way is the best. Leave no loopholes; make sure that you have eliminated other points of view as viable, leaving your solution as the best choice.

This is an excellent approach for analytical people who love to evaluate all details. It can be overkill for favorable, uninformed, and apathetic audiences if they are not detail-oriented. This approach can work well with hostile and hostile-mixed groups.

Example of the reflective situation:

This starts exactly the same as Motivated Sequence (Problem to Solution).

Problem: The turnover rate at your company among both men and women with young children is far above the national average. I am sure that you agree that we need to reverse this trend, if we are to keep our key employees.

Agreement of Criteria: I think that to make a good decision, we need to consider cost, liability, and convenience. Do you agree? Are there others you think we should add? Let's evaluate the available solutions.

Solution #1: Do nothing.

> Advantages:
> • Easiest thing to do
> • Will help with trouble attracting new hires
>
> Disadvantages:
> • Won't solve the problem
> • Turnover rate is critical

Given the disadvantages, we can't afford to do nothing.

Solution #2: Pay for off-site day care.

> Advantage:
> • Liability criteria met
>
> Disadvantages:
> • Cost prohibitive to most employees
> • Totally inconvenient

Again, this won't work. Let's look at another possibility.

Solution #3: Build an on-site day care.

Disadvantage:
• Liability will be an issue

Advantages:
• Our attorney says we can overcome liability
• Convenience and economic benefit for employees

Call to action: I recommend, given the criteria, that we agree building an on-site day-care facility to stop the turnover rate and help us attract quality workers is our best solution. Who will join me to set up a task force to move forward?

Persuasive Presentation Planning Sheet
Reflective

Persuasive   *Reflective*

Central Theme:

Consider: Purpose, Audience, and Logistics (PAL™)

Problem Definition:

Criteria For Judging Possible Solutions:

Possible Solution:

Positives:

Negatives:

Transition

Possible Solution:

Positives:

Negatives:

Transition

Possible Solution: (presenter's choice)

Negatives:

Positives:

INTRODUCTION 10 - 15%

Grabber:

Source Credibility:

WIIFT:

Preview (optional):

CONCLUSION 5 - 10%

Review:

Memorable statement:

Three Models Of Persuasive Speaking

Proposition to Proof:
- Grabber statement
- State your proposition
- Proof – Use logic and emotional appeals
- Review – Draw conclusions
- Memorable statement – Ask for what you want

Motivated Sequence:
- Attention
- Need – Identify the pain. If the audience doesn't "feel" the problem, you won't be able to satisfy it.
- Satisfaction – Talk about how your plan satisfies the need. If there are negatives, put them in the middle.
- Visualization – Paint a positive picture of the benefits of your plan.
- Call to action – Get a commitment

Reflective:
- Grabber
- Problem – State the problem. Develop the problem, proving that it is urgent and a solution must be formed. Agree upon a criteria for evaluating the solutions and making a decision.
- Solution – List the solutions, starting with the weakest. Evaluate each solution against the criteria which was agreed upon. Discuss the positive aspects first, then hit the negatives. The negatives must outweigh the positives. After each solution has been smashed, put it to rest. End with the solution you want. Start with any negatives, then end with the positive elements of your solution and why it

best meets the criteria.

• Review – Do a mini problem-to-solution reinforcing the benefits of your plan.

• Memorable statement – Ask for what you want.

Part Four

What You Need to Know About Making & Using Visual Aids

"People who keep it simple the longest are the most successful."
– **Kirk McCaskill,** former pitcher, Major League Baseball

Our ability to retain information increases by almost 40 percent when visual aids are used. As a presenter, that means you have a greater opportunity to make an impact on your audience.

Proper use of visual aids allows complicated information to be broken down into parts, making it easier for audience comprehension. The speaker also benefits, allowing you to move during your presentation and help the audience stay focused. However, remember that the visuals are an aid, not the presentation! You may well decide visual aids are not necessary. In fact, the best visual is a really good speaker. Remember to use the aid as a tool for the audience – not you as the speaker!

Choosing a visual aid

More often than not, however, most corporate presentations incorporate some type – or types of – visual aids. Modern technology offers you a wide variety of visual aids. For a simple staff meeting, a flip chart can work well. For sales presentations, you can use computer projection systems. To determine which method works best for you, practice using a few different types before you make a final decision. You may wish to use more than one type of visual aid during your presentation, for example: flip charts, handouts and props, or slide shows (PowerPoint, etc.) and videos.

You may find that the type of visual aid you choose depends upon several variables:

- the length of your presentation
- the audience size
- the logistics of the meeting room
- the available equipment
- the type of presentation you will be giving

Don't get so comfortable using one type of visual aid that you are reluctant to try anything else. Even a presentation that you may have given 50 times can take on new life by changing the type of visual aids. You also need to be so prepared that you can still speak if the electricity goes out or the visuals fail.

Types of Visual Aids

Video systems

Video systems can be used for a variety of purposes --
playback of prerecorded tapes, DV minis, and DVDs,
computer-controlled presentations using video monitors or projectors, live video of remote events, and
recording and playing during a presentation. Because
video systems usually involve several pieces of equipment, planning, prechecking, and rechecking are
essential. Keep in mind that if you are not bringing
your own equipment with you, video playback systems
vary. Make sure the format of the tape or DVD you are
using is compatible with the playback machine on site.
Check the compatibility before attempting to play anything. An on-site inspection of the equipment and the
room will save you from embarrassing problems later.
Cameras are changing rapidly, getting away from tapes
and using CDs, DVDs, and DV minis. If you will be
recording as well as using playback, make sure you have
made your requirements known when requesting the
equipment.

Monitors

What size monitor should you use to make sure everyone in the room can see properly? Here are some general guidelines:

Audience size	Monitor size
10 or under	19 inches
11–25	25 inches
26–75	4 to 6 feet

For larger audiences, several large monitors (IMAX) are necessary.

Multimedia: PowerPoint & other software

Many software programs allow your computer to display digital video sequences, transport your audience to out-of-sequence slides or even incorporate other presentations. Multimedia presentation computer packages can include drawing tools for graphics creation, and pre-scripted buttons that can be set to trigger internal events such as starting a video sequence.

If you are going to use an entry-level multimedia presentation package, most of the software available can produce transition effects (wipes, dissolves, etc.) and moving-typeface-style animations that let you sequentially march topics onto the screen. You will also be able to incorporate movies into your slides using programs for either Macintosh® or PC. In addition, some programs incorporate hypertext-like features that can provide interaction with your presentation. Depending on the needs of your audience, you can alter the content of your presentation on the fly. There are also entry-level programs conceived from the outset to integrate text, graphics, audio, animation and video elements into well-coordinated presentations. Because these software packages are constantly changing, it's best to get as much information as possible before purchasing one.

Many Web sites offer speakers a wealth of resources to jazz up their presentations. Here are a few sites: **www.effectivemeetings.com** (insight into how to plan meetings), **www.microsoft.com/office/powerpoint** (great site to visit for how-to articles and tech support); **www.digitaljuice.com** (to purchase a great product called Digital Juice for PowerPoint), and **www.daily-wav.com** (to find interesting sounds and voices for more relaxed special occasion presentations).

Professional speaker and author Tom Antion, whose section on using humor in presentations begins on page 221, says, "A typical problem I see with presenters that use PowerPoint or other computer-based presentations is that they forget to reboot before the presentation. Many conscientious speakers practice their presentation just prior to the actual delivery. They use up many of the computer resources before their actual presentation, and when the time comes to deliver the program, their computer crashes." He also adds, "People don't know their equipment well enough. You must set your computer so that no screen saver or power savers come on. You must know how to get your projector out of 'sleep mode' when necessary. Sometimes two computers are attached to the same projector, so you must know how to switch between the two when it's your turn to present."

Flip charts

Flip charts are best used in small, informal groups. You can write as you speak, or list your points in advance of the meeting. You can add points as your meeting progresses. A flip chart can look sloppy by the end of your presentation, and it can be hard to go back to a previous point unless you tear off the pages and post them around the room.

There are also electronic flip charts, also known as whiteboards. The use of these large electronic flip charts better enables a large group of participants to see the visual aids. When used by remote speakers, whiteboards can allow for real-time interaction with audience members – they "write" notes on them that all can see (and print).

When writing on a standard flip chart, use large letters (2 to 4 inches high); blue or black markers are easiest to read. Never use red and green together. Many people are colorblind and cannot see these colors. They will not be able to differentiate your points. Follow the 4 x 4 rule: use no more than four lines, and four words per line, on any flip chart page. Write only on the top three-fourths of the page. Some presenters write their points very lightly in pencil, in advance of presentations. Then, during the presentation, they are able to write over their points with marker. This is also good for diagrams and graphs. When presenting from flip charts, be sure to stand on the correct side. If you are

Visual Aids -- What NOT To Do

Don't turn your back to the audience.

Don't stand in front of the projection light, blocking participants' view of the visual aid.

Visual Aids -- What To Do

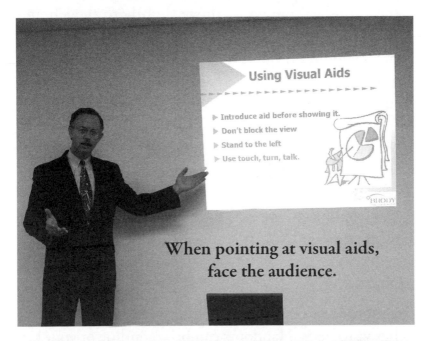

When pointing at visual aids,
face the audience.

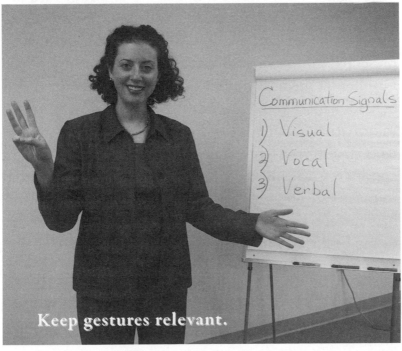

Keep gestures relevant.

right-handed, the flip chart should be to your left. When you begin to write, move slightly to the left and you will be in the correct position. Left-handed presenters should do the reverse. Remember the **three T's – touch, turn and talk** – as you use your visual aids. You are speaking to the audience, not to the flip chart. After you touch your key point, turn to the audience, establish eye contact with someone, and continue to talk. Use the hand closest to the flip chart when touching it. If possible, attach the finished pages to the walls so the audience can see what has already been discussed. You will also be able to add things if needed.

Handouts

Handouts can have copies of charts, slides or graphs or other visual aids. Handouts can be an outline of your key points, or contain information you have chosen not to mention in your presentation. They should be neat, well-presented and have your name, address, and telephone number on them (if you would like your audience members to contact you). They can also contain biographical information about you, and may give some background facts about your company or service. The purpose of handouts is to enhance your speech, not detract from it, so make sure they are clear and readable. Audience members can also be given a disk that contains your handouts, or can be directed to download them from your Web site.

Use handouts when:
- your speech contains a lot of technical information

- you can't put all the information in your speech
- you want an audience to have the choice of taking notes
- you want added value for your audience

Make sure to tell the audience what information is available in the handout, so they can decide when, or if, to take copious notes. If you don't want them to read the handouts during your presentation, give them out at the end.

Guidelines for constructing visual aids

When preparing your visual aids, remember that their purpose is to enhance your presentation, not detract from it. What you are going to say is, obviously, the most important aspect, but good visuals will help you capture and hold your audience's attention. When writing your visuals, remember the following points:

Typeface. Choose one that is easy to read. Sans-serif type is ideal for headlines, serif is better for text (sans serif lacks "feet"). Be consistent and use the same font for all titles, and the same for all text. Don't use more than two fonts. Use a minimum of 18- to 22-point-size boldface type.

Keep it simple. Reading too many words will tire your audience. Use words only to describe your points and summarize when possible. Save the complicated information for your presentation and handout. Use pictures and other graphics instead of words, if possible.

Be consistent. On a single visual, if your bulleted points are in the form of questions, keep them all in question style. If they are in the form of statements, keep them that way.

Titles. Limit the title of a visual to one line and subtitles to two lines. Don't put the title of the program on every visual, they will begin to look cluttered.

Capitalization. Do not capitalize all words. IT'S TOO DIFFICULT TO READ. Use initial capitals for titles. Capitalize any proper names.

Graphs & charts enhance visual aids

Graphs

Simply constructed graphs and charts help an audience grasp your point, make comparisons, or view specific items in relation to the whole. *Profile graphs* use shading underneath the data, and make it easy to see large or significant changes. *Bar graphs* let your audience see blocks of information, allowing them to quickly make visual comparisons. Use a bar graph (or column chart) when you want your audience to focus on the actual figures, not any trends – these best illustrate relative quantities. *Line graphs* (aka "fever charts") make it easy to illustrate trends, to compare over a long time, and show increases or decreases in a quick way. They are usually best to illustrate a growth point or movement, not an actual analysis of the numbers. *Pictographs* use pictures, rather than a line or a bar, to show the same type of information. *Circle graphs* can be used to show proportions of a whole.

Charts

Flowcharts show a series of sequences or relationships in an easy-to-follow format. They are effective for illustrating a process through steps or stages. *Pie charts* clearly depict pieces (or "wedges") in relation to the whole ("pie") and to one another; they are a way to simplify a combination of details. They are good for showing as many as seven sections, such as financial spending. *Organizational charts* help to clarify complex subjects or procedures. They are useful to detail social groups/relationships, or chains of command. They can help your audience quickly see and understand your subject.

Line Drawings

These visual aids work well when a basic process is being described, or to show an aspect of something in detail.

Profile Graph

1 Hour Averages. Dates: All. Days of Week: All

Figure Bar Graph

Line Graph

Average Daily Temperature for January 1-7 in Degrees Fahrenheit

Pictograph

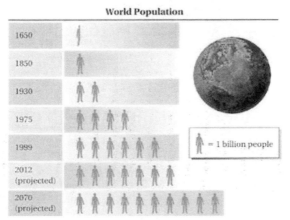

Flow Chart

Figure 1: Part of an example flow chart showing how to route incoming phone calls

Pie Chart

Organizational Chart

4 tips for chart design

- **Make headings active, not passive** (i.e. "Results of Incentive Contests" is better than "1999-2007 Sales").
- **Use basic colors** (avoid colors like blue and green, since colorblind people can't see them) **and big, bold fonts** so the entire audience can read the visual aid.
- **Keep your chart easy to read,** not packed with data. The viewer only has a few seconds to grasp your point.
- **Remember, consistency works.** If the presentation

  has an overall graphic design (template), make sure all charts match this style.

Visual aids need to be planned, executed, and used wisely. Your audience and topic will help you determine which type of visual aid to use. The location of your presentation may dictate the method you choose. Always make sure you have verified the available equipment and power supply before deciding which type of visual aid to use. If possible, have a backup system with you just in case.

Be prepared to give your presentation without visual aids. After all, things go wrong with even the best prepared events.

19 rules to remember when using visual aids

1. Visual aids should be simple enough for the audience to understand the concept in less than 20 seconds.

If the material is complex, do a gradual build – start with an easy-to-understand point and work up to the more complex.

2. Leave the visual aid up long enough for your audience to look it over before you begin talking about it.

3. Don't make visuals so complicated that the audience has to keep reading while you are talking.

4. Don't talk to the screen, talk to the audience. Stand so that the visual aid is to your left. Point with your left hand, which should be closest to the screen when you begin to speak. We read from left to right, so we want to point to the beginning of the sentence.

5. Practice with visual aids before your presentation to get comfortable working with them and the equipment, and, if possible, do so on site.

6. If something goes wrong with the visual aids or equipment, keep going. Turn the machine off, if necessary, and proceed without any visual aids. Remember: The visuals are an aid for the audience, not you, so be able to present without them.

7. When using PowerPoint, get familiar with the "B"

key. Hit the "B" key when you want the screen to go blank. The audience then turns all attention to the speaker. You can hit "B" again when you want to go back to the point on the screen. Many of the newer remotes have the "B" built in already.

8. Arrive early – get the equipment working and in focus. This includes your remote control to change slides.

9. Place your equipment so the screen is to the left of where you'll stand, unless there are two screens or a large screen at least 7 feet off the floor. Visibility is key. Check visibility in the corners and the back row of the room.

10. Avoid standing in the light when something is projected on the screen.

11. Bring extension cords, power surge protectors and cables you might need.

12. Bring duct tape and scissors to secure wires to the floor and walls, so no one will trip.

13. Be sure your power pack is fully charged or new batteries have been installed.

14. Carry an auxiliary light with you, or request one if the room will be darkened.

15. If you are using a modem, verify that the room has

compatible phone jacks and that they work.

16. Have your slides on a memory stick, or bring a back-up CD, DVD, or Zip disk, which can be used in someone else's computer.

17. Make a list of your slides and number each. If you want to skip a few slides, simply hit the number of the slide you want to show, then push "enter." It will go to the slide you selected.

18. Make sure everything is spelled correctly, especially customers' names and products.

19. If renting or borrowing equipment, make sure you are familiar with it before your presentation.

Remember -- a good visual aid doesn't make up for a poor presentation. Don't depend on your visuals to carry you -- they should only be thought of as a reinforcement tool. Be prepared to speak without them just in case!

Part Five

The Three Main Parts of Your Presentation

"Every time I play, in my own mind I'm the favorite."
-- Tiger Woods

Most presentations can be organized into three main parts: the introduction, the body and the conclusion.

The Introduction

Your introduction should tell the audience members what you are going to be talking to them about. If you will be speaking for 30 minutes, your introduction should last for approximately three or four minutes, about 10 percent of your presentation.

The introduction is your chance to make a dynamic first impression, and as the saying goes, "There are no second chances to make a first impression."

Your introduction will serve four purposes:

1. Get the audience's attention
2. Establish WIIFT (What's In It For Them)
3. Establish your credibility and create rapport
4. Let the audience members know where you are going with the presentation and when they can ask questions

Get the audience's attention

You must grab your audience's attention right away. If you start out slowly, you may never get audience members' attention. The best way to focus attention on you is by using a grabber statement or hook to reel them in. This can take many forms. You can tell a story, give an example, ask a hypothetical question, make a controversial statement, use a quote, or use humor. Here are some examples of grabbers that will surely get an audience's attention.

Ask a question

If your speech is about a new substitute for butter, you might begin with this question: "How many of you miss eating butter because you are afraid of having too much fat in your diet?" or, "Would you be willing to try a new food that tastes exactly like butter, but has no fat in it at all?" By asking a question, you give your audience something to quickly think about. In this case, audience members are thinking, "What could really taste like butter, but not contain any fat?"

State an unusual fact

Sticking with the butter substitute, you might start with a statistic like this: "There are 65 butter substitutes on the market, and not one of them really tastes like butter or has no fat at all."

Give an illustration, example or story

Paint a mental picture for your audience members by telling them a story that relates to your subject. This will get their attention and make the content real for them. For example: "Our company has spent the past 25 years trying to create a substitute for butter which actually tastes like the real thing, but has no fat at all. We have finally succeeded."

Use a quotation

Catchy phrases and quotes can be great openers as long as it's not a quote that has been overused. Go to the library or search the Internet for unusual quotes, or quotes from unusual people.

Use humor

If you are going to try humor, be sure it is in good taste and relevant to your speech. Also be sure that you are comfortable using humor, and it's funny. When in doubt, try it out on someone you trust. Using humor in front of a large audience is very tricky; you don't know who you might offend. Humor does not translate well between cultures or even between regions. What's funny in your town might be offensive to the people where you are speaking. Humor at someone's expense is never funny. When in doubt, leave it out.

WIIFT (What's In It For Them)

Don't wait very long to get to this point, or you will lose your audience's attention very quickly. If audience members have been told to attend your presentation, or if they are there reluctantly, they will be fidgeting in their seats until they find out whether or not there is some benefit for them in your presentation. If you haven't convinced them in the first few minutes of your presentation that they will derive some benefit, you will have an almost impossible task ahead of you. Pique their interest quickly.

Let them know who you are

If everyone in the room already knows who you are, you can skip this step. If not, you need to establish your credentials and credibility early on. Let them know why they should be listening to you. Talk about yourself in relation to the topic you will be speaking about. When someone introduces you and lists your credentials, don't repeat them. Give the audience some reasons to want to listen to you. Although I have been introduced many times, I always try to add something at the beginning of my speech that wasn't part of the introduction. Sometimes I refer to something that might have just happened to me, or an experience that sets the tone for my presentation. If you are speaking at a big conference or meeting and you will be introduced, prepare your own introduction and send it to the person who will be introducing you. Bring an extra copy to the event. Ask the person to read what you wrote -- that way you get the setup you want.

Preview your subject

Although your audience members probably know the title or theme of your presentation, and may have a general idea of what it is about, it will help them to hear from you what you are going to be talking about. If you are giving an informative presentation, tell the audience what you want to accomplish. Be direct and keep it short. You can list several of the points you will be covering, and build up to where you want them to go during your presentation. If your goal is to persuade, you do not have to be quite so specific. It's always a good idea for you to tell the audience members when you will take questions. The perfect time to tell them is in the preview.

What you want to avoid in the introduction is: "Good morning, my name is _____, and I am so glad to be here talking to you today about _____." Audience members either know your name or don't care. Besides, when speakers start, the first few seconds are lost because the audience isn't quite listening yet. "I am glad to be here – they don't care! They are here for themselves, not for you. "I will be talking about..." Audience members also know that. Use the opening to break their preoccupation, get them excited because your presentation hits their needs, and you want to create rapport – all before giving them the content. The opening is the most important part of a presentation.

The Body

The body of the presentation (about 80 to 85 percent of your time) is when you tell audience members what you are going to tell them – and the reason you are there! Divide your material into three to five main points. Then, support each point with the data (not just facts and figures). Connect the main points with transitions. When planning your presentation, think of it as an accordion – it can expand or contract depending on timing, and what happens at the event.

The method of organization you choose for the body of your presentation will be determined by the type of presentation, and which best meets your objectives. In the body, you will answer the audience member's question "WIIFM?" (What's In It For Me?). The body of your presentation will contain elements to satisfy both the emotional and logical needs of the audience. It may contain new material and/or material that may be familiar but is presented in a new way. Be selective. Not all of the information you have is important enough to be included. It is worthwhile to keep idea files. Whenever you find a newspaper, magazine or journal article, or hear something you would like to remember, put it into this idea file. Don't trust your memory. I was once told a story that was so incredible, I wanted to use it in a seminar I was leading later that week. I didn't write it down, because I was sure I would remember it. The day of the seminar, I went blank on the story and couldn't tell it to the class. That night, I called the person who told me the story, asked her to please repeat it, and wrote it down. It's a story I still tell in my seminars, but it's written down in my files "just in case." Avoid books which have "speaker stories." Instead, use your own experiences. No one else can tell them!

You can jazz up your presentation by using one or more of the following:

• Examples – add interest
• Stories
• Quotations – must be a well-known and reputable source to have value
• Definitions – can help you prove a point or make a point easier to understand
• Comparisons – present similarities
• Contrasts – present differences
• Statistics – numerical facts and figures supporting your points
• Analogies
• Metaphors
• Humor
• Audience involvement
• Visual aids

Using transitions

To achieve continuity as you move from one part of your presentation to another, use transitional phrases. These are short remarks that will move you from the introduction to the body of your presentation, and from the body to the conclusion. You also use them to move from point to point within the presentation. Transitional phrases should be written out. Helpful transitional phrases are "Now that we have looked at ... let's move on to ..." or "We have established the criteria for ... we can now look at ..."

Using supporting materials in the body

Although you may not be able to convince a hostile audience that your town would benefit by building a skateboard park, using supporting materials can help you go a long way toward making your point. Begin to collect information as soon as you have selected your topic. Write down everything you know on the subject, what are the main points, and what do you need to find out. Be sure that your data is current and accurate. Get as much information as possible to support your position. People remember stories and examples more than data. Use both to reinforce ideas.

Validate your point of view

Although it may be a hard sell to convince taxpayers of your town that a skateboard park is worthwhile, facts and statistics that back up your point of view can help to persuade a skeptical audience of the validity of your arguments. Use facts that parallel your situation. If a nearby community with a similar tax structure has built a skateboard park, and if that community has had significant benefits, outline them in your speech. Have accidents caused by – and to – skateboarders decreased because they are off the town streets and in a safe location? Have homeowners benefited from safer streets? These are the kinds of supporting facts that can help you to strengthen your presentation.

Add interest

Using tax money to provide recreational facilities that primarily benefit only certain children is not an easy sell. Using data will add interest: The number of families who have children that skateboard. The number of accidents caused by unsafe skateboarding. The nuisance to local shopowners and homeowners. The fear of hitting a skateboarder when driving in your town. The low cost of building a skateboard park, compared with the cost of auto and medical bills caused by skateboarding accidents.

Audience involvement

Make the audience part of your presentation by using the data to involve them. For example, when speaking about building a skateboard park, you could ask audience members, "How many of you have children who skateboard or have friends who skateboard?" or "How many of you would feel safer driving around town with skateboarders off the streets?" After seeing their response, you could then quote the statistics of what happened in towns where skateboard parks have already been constructed. Other ways to involve members of an audience include: using their names, asking rhetorical and real questions; using their examples; having them do something.

Look for an emotional connection

If you were to give a presentation on home fire safety, your points would be remembered if you mentioned published stories of losses that occurred in your area when smoke detectors were not installed or not working in the home. Examples of stories and people who make events memorable can help you to make your own presentation memorable. People tend to respond first to emotion, then justify with logic.

Must Know, Should Know, Could Know

Since most presentations run longer than speakers anticipate, be prepared to cut some material if needed. An easy way to accomplish this is to put your information into three categories: Must Know, Should Know, Could Know. Choose a different color marker for each section, so you know immediately which section to eliminate if needed. On your outline, put a box around the "Could Know" section, so you can eliminate it first if necessary. Don't speak faster to try and get all the information in. It will make your audience members nervous, and in your hurry you may confuse them or leave out important information. With planning ahead, you will be prepared in the event you have to shorten your presentation.

The Conclusion

The last 5 to 10 percent of your presentation is the conclusion. It is when you tell the audience members what you have told them. This is the last thing the audience will hear, and possibly remember. It should neatly tie together everything that came before. Be sure to review your main points, or include a strong call to action if you want audience members to do something as a result of your speech. Inexperienced or nervous presenters often miss their final – and possibly best – opportunity to make their point with the audience or ask for a call to action.

An effective conclusion should emphasize the key points made earlier in your presentation. If you have been giving a sales presentation, this is the time to repeat the product benefits and the benefits to the customer if he or she buys your product. If you have been motivating taxpayers to fund a skateboard park, this is your last chance to call them to action and have them sign your petition. Your conclusion should also provide closure to your presentation, and end by giving the audience something to remember. The famous conclusion to John F. Kennedy's inaugural address in 1961, is one of the most quoted historical statements: "Ask not what your country can do for you, ask what you can do for your country." Short, to the point and memorable.

Your closing may not be as memorable as JFK's, but it should have an impact on your audience.

When creating your own memorable close, follow the examples used in the opening: ask a question; state an unusual fact; give an illustration, example or story; or present a quotation. If you use your opening grabber, add a new ending or insight. For example: "If you want your streets and your children to be safer, support the statistics presented here tonight, and vote, 'Yes' on the new skateboard park."

Guidelines for effective conclusions

- Draw conclusions for the audience
- Suggest action or next steps
- Ask for a commitment
- Keep it 10 percent or less of your presentation
- Write it out and really practice it
- End your conclusion on a positive note
- Test your conclusion by asking yourself these questions:
    1. Does my conclusion help listeners get to where I want them to be?
    2. Does it help finish my presentation instead of leaving audience members unsure of what I intended them to know or do?

If the answers to these questions are "yes," then your conclusion meets the criteria for success.

Ten Steps To An Organized Speech

1. Select the topic. Make sure it appropriate for the audience. (Remember your PAL™).
2. Limit the topic to one central theme. Keep in mind the amount of time you have to make your presentation and the level of the audience you will be addressing.
3. Gather the information. Write down everything you know about the topic, then evaluate what you need to research. Remember to include more than just facts and figures – use examples, stories, analogies, case studies, quotes and humor.
4. Outline your main points. Use between three and five main points in the body of your speech to support your central theme. Add transition sentences to connect the ideas.
5. Collect supporting data. Enhance key points with interesting secondary information to help your audience retain information. This is the time to create visuals to reinforce your key points.
6. Design the introduction. Include a grabber or hook to get their attention. Make sure it's catchy and tells audience members WIIFT (What's In It For Them). It's also the time to tell the audience members when you will take their questions.
7. Write a strong conclusion. Lead the audience by referring to your introduction, reviewing key points or delivering a call to action.
8. Put together a final draft. Outline your speech on

note paper using large print (avoid index cards; they are hard to use in a presentation). Use only the top two-thirds of each page and leave room in the margins for notes. Use either single words, sentences, or short phrases. Write out your memorable phrases and transitions.

9. Practice your presentation three to six times out loud. Say it differently each time to keep the spontaneity. Record your practice and make any necessary changes.

10. Practice again in front of an audience similar to the real audience. Practice the questions and answers. Remember: Practice does not make perfect, it makes permanent. Perfect practice makes perfect.

Sample Speech Outline (Speech to Convince)

Audience: Residents of Newark, New Jersey. Favorable mix (favorable, uniformed, apathetic).

Purpose: After hearing my speech, the audience will understand why the police Vest-A-Cop program is so important, and believe it is necessary.

Logistics: 30-minute speech, early morning meeting, overhead projector.

I. Introduction

    A. In cities with Vest-A-Cop programs, police officer fatalities and injuries have been significantly reduced.

    B. Newark has had a Vest-A-Cop program for

three years, and police are very enthusiastic about it.

C. In prior years, many officers were injured. In the five years before the Vest-A-Cop program, six officers were fatally wounded.

D. This program is working very well in Newark.

II. Body

A. Your tax dollars pay for some of the vests.
    1. Tax revenue accounts for 50 percent of funds.
    2. Newark residents' personal donations fund 25 percent of the program.
    3. Fund-raising efforts pay the balance.
B. An added benefit to the residents of Newark as a result of the program has been a reduced crime rate in the city.
    1. Violent crime has gone down.
    2. Police officers are able to patrol on foot more frequently since they got the vests.

Transition: Now that we have seen how beneficial the Vest-A-Cop program is for both officers and citizens, we should consider expanding the program.

C. Newark should be proud of its success; can we improve on our current statistics?
    1. Our police force is safer; now we are safer.
    2. Expanding the program to our suburbs is something to evaluate.

Transition: The Vest-A-Cop program currently costs

each taxpayer $1.50 per year. A police officer out on disability leave costs each of us $25 per year. Vest-A-Cop benefits everyone: We are doing something beneficial for our officers, our community, and ourselves.

    D. It is far less expensive for us to fund additional Vest-A-Cop programs than to pay out disability for each injured officer, or risk officers' lives.
        1. An additional program would cost taxpayers another 50 cents per year.
        2. More well-protected police may further reduce our crime statistics.
        3. No downside.

III. Conclusion (review and memorable statement)

    A. Like its counterparts in other parts of the country, Newark's Vest-A-Cop program is a huge success.
    B. I am asking you to sign a petition to support a Vest-A-Cop program.

Writing Your Final Draft

You have now spent a considerable amount of time organizing your presentation. The purpose is clear, you have completed an audience analysis and you know what the logistics of the speaking situation will be. It's time to construct the final draft of your speech.

I recommend the following format for your final draft:
1. Use 8 1/2 x 11 inch paper – stiff stock – not index

cards, as they tend to get mixed up and are hard to read.

2. Write on only the top two-thirds of the page, so your eyes don't move down or you drop your chin, which makes your voice go down.

3. To make the final draft readable, use at least 18-point font size, bold letters. Or, if you are hand writing it, use a medium point felt-tip pen rather than a ball-point pen.

4. Decide where to use visual aids; make notes in the margins of your draft, and number each visual.

5. Color code your presentation: must know, should know, could know.

Your outline may consist of single words, or it may be in the form of sentences that provide more information. The drawbacks to these forms are with single words, you may forget what you want to say and with sentences, you may start reading them exactly as written. A better choice is to use short phrases that have enough information to keep your speech on track and not enough to cause you to read them verbatim. You can write out your opening grabber, your transitions and any facts or figures you must include, along with the final close. Once you have written your final draft, practice your speech to check for the following:

• Is it clear? • Is it concise? • Is it complete?

Part Six

Practice & Delivery Styles

"They pay me to practice. Sundays I play for free."
-- **Greg Buttle,** former New York Jets linebacker

Practice makes permanent! I have heard thousands of presentations -- in my corporate programs and at conferences. Given equally well-prepared materials, what separates the good presenters from the rest?

They practice! Just like an athlete before any event, or an actor before a performance, so, too, should a speaker practice. Even the most interesting speech will fall flat if it isn't delivered well. And the primary reason that happens is not practicing properly -- or practicing enough. Here is how I recommend you practice:

• Practicing in your head isn't practicing. We are all quite eloquent in our minds. However, when we speak out loud something entirely different comes out. The only way to practice correctly is to practice aloud.

- Practice your presentation differently each time you do it. This will help you keep the spontaneity, and help you be prepared for last-minute changes. The goal is to keep it conversational.
- If your presentation is complicated or technical, practice saying it to a spouse or friend who is most like your intended audience to gauge how easy the material is to understand.
- After practicing several times, try practicing just the rough spots. Try those along with your opening and closing statements, key points, and transitions until you are comfortable with them.
- Practice in the same way you will be presenting. If you will be standing, then stand. If you will be seated, sit.
- Tape record yourself after you have practiced out loud several times. As you listen, ask yourself if you would enjoy this presentation if you were a member of your audience. If you wouldn't, it's time to re-write and practice again. Work on your timing.
- Practice with your visual aids. During your last few practice sessions, use whatever aids or handouts you will be using during your presentation. This serves as a final check of whether you have too many visuals or not enough. There is still time for you to change things and make final adjustments. You also need to be familiar with the equipment.
- Do a dress rehearsal. Set up an area with a similar seating arrangement. If possible, try to have a live

audience or at least one person who is similar to your real audience. Give your entire presentation, including taking questions from the "audience." Ask for feedback and make any last-minute corrections.

• Use every opportunity to practice. A perfect time is when you are driving in the car. You can speak out loud and play audio tapes you have made of your practice sessions.

A timing tip for practice

Typically, unless they tend to race through a presentation, presenters go over their allotted times or rush the ending of their speech. This can destroy a meeting agenda, or be unfair to audience members and other speakers. Practice can help to get the timing right.

Follow this formula:

75% rule of thumb: If the presentation does not include interruptions, interaction or questions, practice to go for 75% of the allotted time (prepare and practice your presentation to last 45 minutes for a 60-minute time frame).

Almost inevitably, the presentation will end up taking the full hour. The worst thing that could happen is that you will be finished early -- and no one complains about that! You can also allow time for questions at the end without rushing.

50% rule of thumb: If you include a few questions and some interaction, plan, prepare and practice the presentation to last for 50% of the allotted time (30 minutes for a 60-minute presentation).

25% rule of thumb: If your presentation is highly interactive, like in a training or sales situation, limit your talk to 25% of the allowed time period.

When preparing your presentation, remember to categorize your material into the must know, should know and could know categories. That way, you can take out material throughout the practice session, and even during the actual delivery.

Use a clock during practice and write notes on your outline about the amount of time each section actually represents -- not how much time you think it will take.

Practice on site

If possible, it is advisable to practice your presentation in the room where you will be giving it. This will enable you to check your equipment and get comfortable in the room. If using a lectern, make sure it is placed where you want it. If someone will be speaking before you, note where you want the lectern placed in case it is moved prior to your presentation. Standing behind the lectern for any length of time is not a good idea. It separates you from your audience when your objective is to bring yourself closer to it.

Step out from behind the lectern and move closer to the audience. If you are nervous and need to refer to your notes, walk behind it again when you feel the need. You could also put your notes on a music stand or table. Speakers who spend their entire presentation behind the lectern are perceived as aloof. Speakers of short stature sometimes cling to the lectern because of the riser placed behind it to make them tall enough to be seen. A better choice would be to walk forward and stand closer to audience members. It will help to establish a good rapport with them. If you are forced to stand behind the lectern because that is where the microphone is located, consider requesting the use of a wireless (lavaliere) microphone or buy your own. If you haven't used a wireless microphone before, familiarize yourself with it well in advance of your presentation so you are not fumbling and can turn it off and on with ease. Remember to turn it off as you leave the platform so that any private remarks you may make are not overheard by the audience.

There are several different kinds of microphones on the market. Get comfortable with as many models as you can, as you may not know what is available where you are presenting. Or, bring your own along.

On the day of your presentation:

1. Arrive early and check the room; locate electrical outlets, and test them. Distribute any handouts.
2. Test your equipment. Know how to contact the audiovisual people.
3. If necessary, have telephone calls re-routed or unplug any phones in the room.
4. Locate restrooms.
5. Check seating and rearrange if necessary.
6. Make sure your visual aids can be seen from every seat.
7. Make sure you can be heard from the back of the room.
8. Set up your visual aids, tape wires down if needed.
9. Check the room lighting.
10. Do body warm-ups, stretches, relaxation exercises.
11. Check your appearance; make any adjustments.
12. Greet your audience.

Delivery techniques

Different speaking situations call for different delivery techniques. These techniques are identified as Impromptu, Extemporaneous, Expromptu, Manuscript and Memorized.

Impromptu style

Also known as "off the cuff," impromptu speeches are given on the spur of the moment. Occasions include meetings when you were not previously informed that you would be speaking, or when you are asked to give a status report, comment on a proposal, or just share your opinion about the topic under discussion. Many presentations are impromptu, and you can be prepared to present even when you haven't had any advance notice.

The secret to being successful at impromptu speaking is to relax and let your knowledge of the subject work for you. If you are going to a meeting, come prepared, just in case you may be called upon for your input and opinions. That way it won't come as a surprise when you are asked. When you know your subject well, it is easier to relax and speak. If you even suspect that you may be asked for an opinion, do some homework on the topic being discussed so you will be able to add something of value.

A good example of this would be if you are going to a meeting where the topic is downsizing in your department, and you are fairly certain your opinion will be solicited since you are a mid-level manager. Now is the time to jot down your thoughts and be prepared. If you are asked to speak, you are ready. If someone else speaks first and says the same things you were thinking, you will be able to at the very least agree or disagree and give your reasons why. Many people use impromptu speaking as a way to test their knowledge and the knowledge of colleagues. Successful impromptu speaking offers you an opportunity to shine, and impress colleagues and perhaps your boss. In group situations, impromptu speaking can become brainstorming sessions resulting in new ideas. If you have very strong opinions on a topic, this is a chance for you to be heard. Being succinct, concise, and to the point are critical skills when asked a question or presenting off-the-cuff information.

The next time you are asked to take a position, give an opinion, or state your ideas, rather than talking in circles, rambling or apologizing for not being prepared, remember the pneumonic device PREP – it's a great model to help you with your impromptu speaking.

Here's what to do: Pause first, then ...

P – Give your Point of view, Position or Proposition. You want to begin by answering the question being asked up front. This shows clarity.

R – State your Reason. Why is it you support that position? This is typically filled with facts and figures.

E – Provide an Explanation or Example that more clearly defines, and reinforces, your reason.

P – Finally, conclude by restating your Point of view, Position or Proposition.

For example, if asked, "Which of these three project options do you prefer?," I might say, "I Propose that we should go with Project B. The Reason I say that, is that it will be the easiest and most cost effective to implement. For Example, we did a similar project last year, and it took only 60 days when we thought it would be 90. Also, the project ran 7% under budget. So, my Point of view is that we should go with Project B."

Typically, people give their Point of view and Reason, and then stop short. By giving an Example and Restating your position, you will take your opinion even deeper and give it more validity.

Using the PREP model will have an enormous impact on your listeners. You will appear well organized, which gives you outstanding credibility. The information you provide will sound logical and concise. Overall, you will have enormous clarity and will avoid rambling, plus you'll avoid annoying your audience. In no time at all, PREP will have you impressing everyone with how succinct you are when put on the spot for your opinion.

Extemporaneous style

This is the delivery style most recommended for speakers. Extemporaneous style presentations are planned, prepared and practiced. They are polished presentations which may be given many times, but should never be exactly the same. You may use an outline or notes, but the speech isn't written out or memorized. An extemporaneous speech may sound off the cuff, but it isn't. Each and every detail has been planned in advance – including anecdotes and illustrations used to make your points. Because what you want to say is planned, you are able to change things around to adapt to your particular audience each time the presentation is given. Politicians usually give extemporaneous speeches. For example, they frequently speak on the same subjects, but they tailor their style and anecdotes specifically for the region they are visiting. If they are in an urban area, they use urban examples; in a farm area, rural ones.

Expromptu style

A combination of extemporaneous and impromptu styles of delivery, the expromptu speech is prepared but not practiced. Unfortunately, this happens too often in corporate America. People wait too long to prepare, and then run out of time to practice. Other occasions when you could be asked to give an expromptu presentation may be at a meeting, conference or debate. When you are asked to participate, take some time to put your thoughts together, even though you have no time to practice. Your success as an expromptu speaker depends on how well you gather and organize your thoughts. On these occasions, you still have time to write an opening sentence that will set you up to make your points. Use notes to help organize your thoughts. Write a closing sentence to end your presentation; this will also serve to let your audience know you have finished speaking.

Manuscript style

A manuscript speech is written down and read word for word to the audience. It is widely used in the scientific community, where technical papers requiring exact wording are submitted for approval, accepted and then read by the author. Politicians, and many CEOs, use manuscript speeches when they want their exact words to be used. It is also the style employed by people who use teleprompters.

This format also ensures exact adherence to a timetable that can be essential when each speaker has a limited amount of time available for his or her presentation. You can use visual aids with a manuscript speech to help make it more interesting for the audience. Unless you have to use the manuscript style, it is best to avoid it. If you have material that has to be presented exactly as written, do so, but try to paraphrase the rest of the speech. If you must read from a manuscript, use the scope technique – slide your thumb and pointer finger down the page, scoping one section at a time. This will help you to find your place after you look up at the audience. It is critical that the manuscript is easy to read. Use a combination of upper and lower case letters, fonts that are 24- point size, and mark the script with underlines for key words to emphasize, spaces for pause, etc. Manuscript presentations require a great deal of practice, so they sound conversational and spontaneous.

Memorized style

Unless you are a professional actor who can memorize speeches, and make them sound like you just came up with the thoughts, forget about memorized style presentations. Most people cannot memorize every word they have written. And, there are obvious differences between orally spoken language and written words. Typically, people do not speak the way they write. Oral language consists of short sentences and phrases, contractions, slang, and starts and stops. Written language consists of longer, more formal sentences with transitions. What reads well doesn't always sound good.

The most painful public speaker to watch is one who has written a speech, thinks he or she has it memorized, gets up to the lectern and forgets it. Because of the way the presentation has been prepared, he or she is unable to go on or even come up with an alternate memorized speech. As a speaker, you depend on cues from people in the audience to guide your delivery, adapting it when necessary to meet their needs. It is hard to do this with a memorized presentation.

The five styles of delivery & when to use them

Style	Description	When To Use It
Impromptu	Off the cuff	Spur of the moment, typically at meetings
Extemporaneous	Planned, prepared, practiced	When you know you have a presentation to give
Expromptu	Prepared, not practiced	Meetings, short notice
Manuscript	Written, read word for word	Scientific and political conferences (when exact wording is critical), and when a speech writer prepares your speech
Memorized	Recited word for word	Never! (unless you are a professional actor)

Part Seven

Stage Fright & How to Control It

"Fear is a huge factor in diving. It's a part of the sport, it's a part of overcoming the sport, it's a part of the thrill of the sport."
-- **Michele Mitchell-Rocha,**
Olympic silver medal winner, diving

You have a problem. You are one of the millions of people who are frightened to speak in public. You are not alone.

Whether this is your first presentation, or number 100, almost everyone suffers from some level of stage fright or performance anxiety. Actors suffer from the same feelings, and many say they never get over them. What they have learned, and what you can learn, is to take those feelings and use them to your advantage. Although in surveys, the fear of speaking in public ranks ahead of death, flying, heights, and snakes, this fear can be controlled. It is a perfectly normal feeling, and a form of energy that can be channeled to your benefit. To use these feelings to your own advantage, first you must identify them. There are six common fears that most speakers have:

1. Fear of your mind going blank. This can happen. We have all seen it happen to other people, and you need to learn what to do if it happens to you: Pause, look at your notes to pick up again where you left off, or move on to your next thought. Don't be afraid to use your notes to get back on track. If you realize a mistake was made during your presentation, correct it if it will have impact on the audience, or let it slide if it is something unimportant. Practice will limit the possibility of your mind going blank.

2. Fear of showing various physical signs of stage fright, including nervousness, trembling or the shakes. What if, despite your best efforts, you still get stage fright? There are many techniques to help you control these physical symptoms. I still get the last-minute jitters many times before addressing an audience. I will go into greater detail later in this chapter about how to address and manage physical symptoms of stage fright. The goal is to never call attention to the physical symptoms. If your focus is more on the audience and not on yourself, the symptoms will begin to dissipate.

3. Someone challenges you and you don't know the answer. It's OK to not know an answer to a question. Just remember: NEVER lie. Be honest, and tell the person you will get back to him or her as soon as possible with an answer, and then follow up as promised. Or, if possible, ask another expert who may be in the audience. You can limit the possibility of not knowing the answer by anticipating the questions – what is the worst question you could get? If you were in the audience, what questions would you ask? Practice the questions and answers. If you are asked questions that you should have known were coming, it means you didn't prepare thoroughly.

4. Fear of being judged and embarrassing yourself. If you are well prepared and have practiced enough, everything should go smoothly. It is important that the audience knows you enjoy your subject, even if you've made some mistakes or have lost your place. A sincere presenter doing his or her best, who is obviously well prepared, and interested in the audience, will not be judged harshly.

5. The audience members think you don't know enough about the subject. If you have backed up your material with facts and figures, and anecdotes to illustrate your points, this shouldn't be a problem. Do your homework!

6. A bad presentation will ruin your reputation. If you haven't prepared thoroughly, or didn't take time to know your audience, a bad presentation may ruin your reputation. If, however, you've done the upfront preparation, and still had some problems in delivery, chances are it won't be as bad as you think. We all have bad days and make mistakes. Most often what you believe to be a major faux pas or a poorly received speech, wasn't as awful as you think. If you do, however, receive negative participation evaluations or bad feedback from the client, address this concern head on. If you show high integrity in this respect to satisfy the client, practice to eliminate any similar, future errors, this one blemish will not ruin your reputation.

Once you have identified your fears, begin working to manage them and let them help you. First, accept that stage fright is a normal feeling, experienced by most people. Next, observe how other speakers handle their anxiety or ask them what they do to relax before a presentation. Perhaps you've noticed speakers doing breathing exercises, or shoulder and head rolls before their presentations. Many speakers have brief exercise routines that help them relax. Others use self-talk to turn the fear into excitement. An important aspect of fear control is to speak frequently. The more you practice, the better speaker you will become.

Self-talk builds self-esteem

The conversations you have with yourself build or destroy your self-image. If you can regulate your self-talk to upgrade your self-image, you can convince yourself of almost anything. If you walk into a presentation believing you are going to fail, you probably will. But if you do as I do, and give yourself a positive self-talk, your chances for success will increase drastically. I frequently use a self-talk mantra. It goes like this: "I'm glad I'm here. I'm glad you're here. I know that I know." I repeat this mantra over and over to myself until I am relaxed. The message you are sending to yourself is one of joy and ease. It expresses your pleasure in being there to present. It says, "I'm thinking about you," and communicates that you have taken the time and effort to prepare a presentation worth giving and listening to. Positive self-talk is an effective means of controlling stage fright.

Visualization

Another effective way to control stage fright is by using visualization. In the visualization process, you picture yourself in front of an audience. You are composed, confident, and in control. You see yourself delivering a presentation, and in your mind's eye, you watch yourself as you successfully reach out to the audience and deliver an audience-centered presentation. You need not go farther than your introduction, but you may want to include a positive response by the audience. By picturing yourself in a successful situation, you are able to give yourself the confidence you need to achieve your goal.

Staying in control

Positive self talk and *visualization* are tools to help you control your stage fright, but there are some basic rules to follow which will make controlling your fears easier.

Arrive early. Get to where you are presenting with lots of time to spare. This will give you a chance to relax, survey your surroundings, make a trip to the restroom, organize your thoughts, and check the facilities -- as well as any equipment you may be using. The speaker who rushes in at the last minute does himself or herself a disservice. We all need the time to mentally prepare ourselves for the event at hand.

Eat lightly. Before you are going to present, it is best to avoid heavy meals. This also means *no alcohol,* and nothing that might cause your stomach to be upset. Bananas are a good choice, they are light and filling – and the potassium will give you necessary energy. It is also important to *avoid taking decongestants or other medications* that might make you drowsy. You don't want to appear tired during your presentation.

Use humor in your presentation to help release endorphins. Laughter is a great tension reliever. This helps you and your audience relax.

Take some of the pressure off yourself by *using interactive techniques.* When you begin your presentation, plan to ask audience members a question and get them to raise their hands. Or, have them brainstorm, or talk to a partner, or do other interactive activities you can think of. This will take some of the focus away from you, and put it onto them. You can use these moments to take a deep breath and relax.

Brody's basics

The "rag doll": Stand up straight with your feet comfortably apart. Stretch up tall, then bend over by collapsing quickly and loosely from the waist with your arms relaxed and hands dangling. Keep your arms, hands, and neck relaxed so you look like a rag doll. Do not bounce. Wait 10 seconds. Now, slowly rise up to a straight position, keeping relaxed. Repeat five times.

Head rolls: Immediately after the rag doll, while your neck is still relaxed, stand straight with your hands close to your chest. Begin to slowly rotate your neck first to the left, then forward with your chin down in front, then to the right. Don't roll your neck back. Reverse the rotation rolling to the right, then front, then left, the front. Be sure your neck is relaxed. Repeat five times.

Arm swings: After the head roll, stand straight with your arms to your sides. Swing your left arm in a large circle from front to back, as if you were doing the back stroke. Swing your right arm in a large circle from front to back in the same manner. Reverse and swing your left arm in a large circle from back to front. Do the same with your right arm. Swing your arms in this manner five times on each side.

Shoulder shrugs: Right after the arm swings, stand straight with your arms at your sides. Using your arms, move your shoulders straight up to the level of your ears. Drop your shoulders back down to their resting position. Shrug your shoulders four more times.

Yawning: After completing the rag doll and the head rolls, your face and neck muscles and vocal chords should be relaxed. Now, standing straight, slowly yawn, sounding an "ahhhhh" on exhalation. The sound you make is a relaxed sound. Strive for this relaxed and open quality whenever you speak.

Abdominal breathing: Sit upright in a chair and place both feet flat on the floor. Rest your hands in your lap. Take a deep breath through the nose while extending your stomach. Push your stomach out as the air, comes into and fills your lungs. Your shoulders can rise, and may possibly go back a bit. Place one hand on your chest and the other on your abdomen. Which hand rises most? If it is the hand on your abdomen, you are breathing properly. If not, pull your breath deeper into your lungs. Once your lungs are full, hold the air to the count of six, and then let the air escape from your nose. Repeat, taking each deep breath slowly through the nose. Do this 10 times.

Brody's refreshers

If you find you need a quick refresher before giving your presentation, here are two that you can do even while seated at your table or on the dais.

Deep breathing I: Take a deep breath in through your nose and tighten everything in your body, from your head, neck, shoulder, hands, fingers, legs and toes. Hold the breath for six seconds, then slowly let go of the tension in your body as you exhale through your mouth to a count of 10.

Deep breathing II: Take a deep breath and clasp your hands together. Hold your breath as you squeeze your palms together tightly. Let go of your hands and breathe at the same time.

Both of these deep breathing refreshers help you to slow your heartbeat. As you do this, you will also slow down the surge of adrenaline that is making you tense.

Final pointers & reminders

1. Accept the fact that stage fright is normal; you may have it every time you speak – but let it work for you by thinking of it as excitement, not fear.
2. Spend your time preparing, not procrastinating.
3. Practice, practice, practice before you are going to present. Remember, perfect practice makes perfect.
4. Speak often; the more you speak, the better you will be able to manage your stage fright.
5. Come with an attitude of service -- not ego! It's about the audience, not you.

Managing the Physical Symptoms of Stage Fright

For dry mouth:
• No milk products, soda, alcoholic beverages, caffeine, sugar

- Lightly coat your teeth with Vaseline™ (petroleum jelly); it will stop your lip from sticking to your teeth
- Bite the tip of your tongue (this helps you to salivate)
- Drink room temperature or warm water (with lemon, if available)

For sweaty hands/body:
- Use talcum powder or corn starch
- Carry a handkerchief

If you have red splotches on your face:
- Wear pink or red colors
- Wear high necklines
- Use humor to release endorphins

If your voice is shaky:
- Project your voice to the back row of the audience

If your hands are shaky:
- Gesture; make them small gestures, don't wave about wildly

If your legs are shaky or your knees are knocking:
- Move about the platform or walk

If your heartbeat is rapid:
- Do some deep breathing

Part Eight
Delivery Dynamics

"The key for me is to forget about the results and concentrate on execution."
-- **Oral Hershiser,** former pitcher, Major League Baseball

The way we deliver our message to other people is made up of three components, what I call the three V's: Visual, Vocal, Verbal. Each carries a percentage of the listener's perception of the total message. These are overall percentages, which can vary based upon the speaker, subject, and audience.

The visual is what we see: dress, grooming, body language, posture, and facial expression. The vocal is your voice, and how it sounds to others. The verbal is the words you choose. These three components are far from equally weighted. Since the visual has the most initial impact, it is important that you as a presenter properly prepare yourself to show your audience a positive visual message.

The Visual
Dress for success

How you look can color what people hear you saying. If you have done your homework and researched the audience, you can choose clothing that will enhance your presentation and be appropriate for the occasion. If you are speaking at a conference, ask the color of the backdrop. Avoid what I did once – wear a royal blue suit only to find a royal blue background. I blended in, and all you could see was a talking head.

For men, a suit demonstrates more authority than a sportscoat or blazer. However, if you are in a warm-weather climate, and many members of the audience are wearing short-sleeve shirts or dressing more casually, a suit may make you seem standoffish.

When unsure of what to wear, ask the person who has scheduled you to speak, or talk to others in the company. For men, dark colors such as navy blue, gray, and black communicate power and authority. For big men, black may seem too austere. Keeping the suit jacket closed gives the impression of a broad chest and narrow waist. White or light-blue shirts are always appropriate, along with silk ties, high-rise socks, and polished dark leather shoes.

Many companies have business casual days. As an outside visitor to the firm, this does not apply to you unless requested to wear business casual attire.

Women do not have to dress like men to appear professional, but they do have to look appropriate. Skirts should not be too short or too tight. Check to see that there are no runs in stockings, and carry an extra, "emergency" pair. Shoes should be conservative, with low- to mid-sized heels. Jewelry should not clang, or dangle. Sweaters should not cling, and blouses should not be low cut.

Find out which colors look best on you and wear them. If you are unsure, a professional image or color consultant is a worthwhile person to consult. Make sure your clothes fit properly. If you wear glasses, save the tinted lenses for weekends. People want to see your eyes when you speak. The day of your presentation is not the time for new shoes, unless you have broken them in first. You don't want to find yourself standing in front of a group with a pained expression because your feet hurt. If you are unsure as to how your clothing looks, have someone view you from all sides – including the rear. Use a full-length mirror to check yourself. Clothing that fits poorly will distract from what you have to say. Audience members may remember your split seam instead of the speech.

Traditional business professional wardrobe, men

- Two-piece *suits*. Several 2-button, 3-button or double-breasted suits in navy, gray, charcoal, or pinstripes. Double-breasted jackets must be buttoned except when sitting down. Suit jackets should not be worn with other trousers.

- *Ties* should be silk. Colors and patterns should not be loud or flashy. Burgundy, red, and navy work as background colors. Small prints and stripes are good choices. Paisleys are good alternatives. Knot should fill the space at the shirt top.
- *Shirts* should be cotton, long-sleeved, even in warm weather. Solid colors are preferred. Shirts should be well pressed. Avoid lavender, peach, plaids, dots and broad stripes.
- Polished, lace-up leather *shoes* in a dark color (black is best).

Business casual wardrobe options, men

- Gaberdine trousers (classic casual).
- Long-sleeve, cotton shirts with sport jackets (classic casual).
- Chino trousers (smart casual).
- Long- or short-sleeve cotton shirts (smart casual).
- Cotton golf shirts with collars (smart casual).
- Sweaters (smart casual).
- Loafers or lace-up shoes with socks (classic and smart casual).
- Leather belts (classic and smart casual).

Traditional business professional wardrobe, women

- Black, navy, burgundy, forest green or gray two-piece skirted suit.
- Pantsuit may work, depending on your industry.
- Two-piece dress or dress with jacket.
- Several neutral blouses or shells -- silk or silk blends.

- One pair each of gold, silver and pearl earrings.
- Scarves that pick up colors from suits or blouses.
- Black, navy or taupe pumps.
- Skin-toned shade of hosiery.

Business casual wardrobe options, women

- Gaberdine, wool and other dress slacks (classic casual).
- Silk shirts with blazer (classic casual).
- Contrasting jacket and skirt (classic casual).
- Pantsuits -- dark or pastel colors (classic and smart casual).
- Cotton shirts in solids, prints or muted plaids (classic and smart casual).
- Low-heeled pumps (classic and smart casual).
- Stockings or socks (classic and smart casual).
- Long or unconstructed skirts (smart casual).
- Chino pants (smart casual).
- Sweaters and sweater sets (smart casual).
- Blazers to wear over slacks or skirts (smart casual).
- Boots and flats (smart casual).

Business Professional
what to wear

pantsuit

skirted-suit

conservative heels

limited jewelry

skirted-suit

well-fitting suit & tie

maternity pantsuit

Business professional is the classic suit. See pages 107-109 for a detailed list of options.

Classic Casual
what to wear

Classic Casual is a step down from Business Professional. The clothing is still structured. Men can take off their ties and wears sports jackets and trousers, rather than suits. Women can wear sweaters and cotton blouses. The jacket (which can be removed) for men and women, is still part of the Classic Casual look.

Smart Casual
what to wear

Smart Casual is a step down from Classic Casual. The jacket is gone. The fabrics can be softer, and less structured. Slacks can be gaberdine or high-quality chino. Women can wear long skirts or slacks. Always wear stockings or socks and closed shoes. Collared golf shirts and sweaters are also appropriate.

Resort Casual
what to wear

Resort Casual is much less formal than business casual. Yet, clothes that are overly tight and show too much skin are still inappropriate. What can work? Men: shorts, chinos, short-sleeved shirts (silk or cotton), even T-shirts. Shoes without socks, sneakers and sandals all work. Women: shorts, slacks, cropped pants, long skirts, sleeveless shirts, flats, sandals, and no stockings all work.

Weekend Wear/Dress Down
(not appropriate corporate attire)

"sexy" tank

Short skirt

Open sandals

T-shirt

sneakers

Avoid these clothes for work. Save them for at home over the weekend. These items include: T-shirts, jeans, sandals and sleeveless tops. Other clothes not appropriate for the work-place: shorts, torn clothing, leggings, sun dresses, cropped clothing, and anything showing too much skin.

Grooming guidelines – men & women

- Clean hair; if you spot dandruff flakes, use tape to remove them before your presentation begins.
- Clean, well-pressed, unspotted clothing, missing buttons or loose hems fixed.
- Clean, clear glasses (no sunglasses indoors).
- No glasses hanging on chains or other devices.
- Polished, clean, white teeth.
- Good breath -- avoid onion, garlic, dairy products.
- Facial hair (and nose hair) trimmed for men, removed for women.
- All buttons buttoned, zippers up, and straps hidden.
- Check a full-length mirror.

Posture is important!

Do you slump or slouch? Have you ever been told to stand up straight? To evaluate your own posture, first look at yourself on video or in photographs. If you don't like the way you look, follow these directions:

- Put your feet hip width apart -- keep them parallel facing the audience. Put your weight on the balls of your feet, which will throw your knees slightly forward. This will keep you from swaying or shifting your weight.
- Put your arms loosely by your sides.
- Now your shoulders are over your hips, your back is lengthening and widening and your posture is straight and good.

When you are seated, you want to look energized and confident. You don't want to lean or slouch or appear too comfortable or relaxed. Proper seated posture when you are presenting (or if you just want to look good at a meeting) is sitting straight up in your chair, spine straight, with your feet flat on the floor and hands open on the table.

Posture and movement

Have you ever watched a speaker sway or rock at the podium? It's very distracting, and can detract from even the most interesting speech. How you appear to audience members will have an impact on their reaction to what you are going to tell them. Your posture and the way you conduct yourself on the platform is an important part of your presentation. You want the audience to see that you are relaxed and in control. To achieve a comfortable speaking position, stand up and spread your feet about 6 to 8 inches apart, parallel to each other with toes pointed straight ahead. Flex your knees and put your weight on the balls of your feet. Standing in this position will stop any swaying or rocking motion and will diminish any distracting heel movements.

Comfortable movements will relax both you and your audience. Take at least two steps, and then get back into position. Do not pace, it's distracting. Use movements to establish contact with your audience. You may even want to walk to the side of the room, pause there, speak, and then return to your place in front.

Getting physically closer to your audience increases its

attention and interest. It also encourages response if you are asking questions. The accepted public distance zone is 12 to 25 feet. In smaller group situations, you can approach within a social distance of 4 to 12 feet primarily, and occasionally get as close as 18 inches to 4 feet. Stand up straight and face the audience head-on. Keep your posture open with arms relaxed and hanging down at your sides. If your arms are crossed in front, it may make you seem defensive. Hold your head high, with your chin up. Having your chin raised gives you the aura of being in control; chin down connotes acquiescence. Visual signals that make you appear not to be in control will detract from your presentation.

The eyes have it

Don't be afraid to make eye contact with audience members; their reactions to you will help your performance as a presenter. If you sense boredom, you may have to pick up the pace; if you sense enthusiasm, it can help to pump you up. When you make eye contact, you are relating to your audience, which will help get your message across.

In order to make proper eye contact, think of the audience as sitting in a "Z" formation. Start with a familiar or friendly face. Look at that person for three to five seconds, or to complete a thought, and then move on to someone else in the room. Don't be predictable. Start in the middle or back of the room to vary your eye contact. If you make eye contact with someone who quickly turns away, try not to look directly into that person's eyes again. In some cultures, direct eye contact is inappropriate, and some people just feel uncomfortable being looked at. You may also nod occasionally, and you will probably get a nod back, at least if the person agrees with what you just said. If you get a head shake, you'll know who disagrees with you.

Facial expressions

Be aware of your facial expressions. Put a mirror next to your desk at work for one week. Watch your face when you are talking on the telephone. Be aware of any artificial, unfriendly, or deadpan expressions you may be making. Do you squint, frown, make strange faces? Once you become aware of the expressions you make, it will be easier for you to eliminate them. Practice smiling and looking pleasant. That's how you want to look during your presentations.

It isn't easy to speak and smile at the same time, but it is important to have an animated expression during your presentation. Make it congruent with your message. Some men find it more difficult to smile while presenting than women do, but practice helps here. Videotape your presentation or practice in front of a friend. Watch your expression and see if you have smiled enough and in appropriate places. If not, you can write reminder notes to yourself in the margin of your speech or just practice smiling beforehand. Women must be careful not to over smile. They may appear to be insipid.

Body language

You're at a meeting and have just been asked for your views. You are unprepared, nervous and want to slump down in your seat so no one will notice you. No matter how nervous you are, now is the time to sit up straight in your chair, keep your hands above the table, use gestures and make eye contact. While you are trying to collect your thoughts, open by paraphrasing the question you have just been asked. This will give you a brief amount of time to think of something to say. Others at the meeting will be responding to your body language. How you look, gesture, and make eye contact will be influencing their opinion. You usually don't get a second chance to make a first impression, so the visual message you send must be strong and positive.

Gestures

Gestures are also a part of your visual picture. They are visual reinforcements of the words and ideas you are trying to communicate to your audience. Gestures include hand, arm, and head movements, and can enhance your presentation or detract from it. Have you ever had a conversation with someone who "talks with their hands?" In some cultures, it is an accepted and commonplace addition to spoken communication. In North American culture, some hand gestures – such as finger pointing and fist raising – can be interpreted as hostile or threatening.

Seated -- What NOT to Do

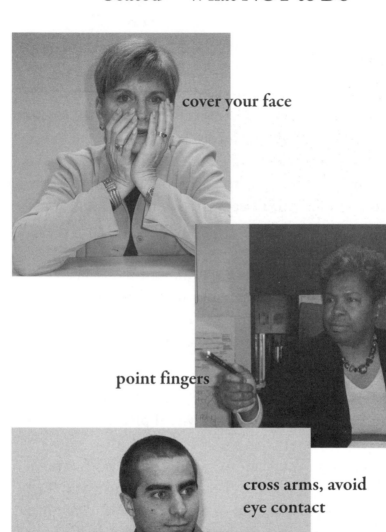

cover your face

point fingers

cross arms, avoid
eye contact

Seated -- What NOT to Do

arms behind head,
foot on table

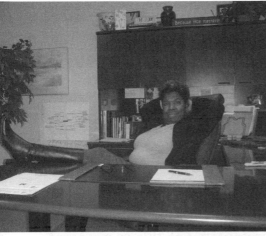

hands in lap

hiding behind
laptop, not pay-
ing attention

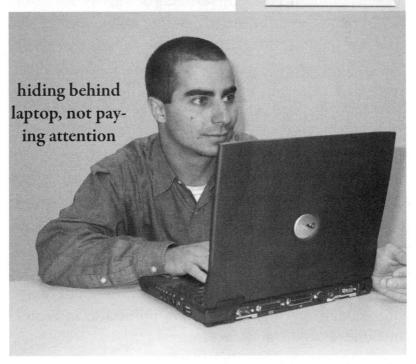

When giving presentations, men often stand in the "at ease" position commonly used in the military. They clasp their hands behind their backs, and they keep them there. Or, they cross their hands low in front of them like a fig leaf on a statue. Both men and women frequently cross their arms over their chests thinking they appear relaxed and confident. To many in the audience, this stance makes the speaker look defensive. By facing audience members with your arms crossed, you are closing yourself to them, and they will sense this. Since your objective is to communicate with openness and sincerity, you want to make open gestures to reinforce what you are saying.

Another gesture to avoid is putting your hands in your pockets. Some nervous presenters use this as a way of keeping their shaking hands out of sight, and often wind up jingling the change in their pocket or their keys, without realizing it. Some people can't get their hands back out again and wind up spilling the contents of their pockets as they try to release their hands. To avoid embarrassment, it's wise to empty your pockets of change and keys before presenting.

Clasping your hands into a folded position, as when praying, is another gesture to eliminate. This gesture tightens you up and pulls in your energy instead of releasing it and allowing you to reach out to the audience. A weak twirling motion with your hands or wagging your fingers when making a point also indicates your unease to the audience.

Gestures -- What NOT to Do

looking down at notes

looking down, "fig leaf"

"parade rest"

"choir girl"

Gestures -- What NOT to Do

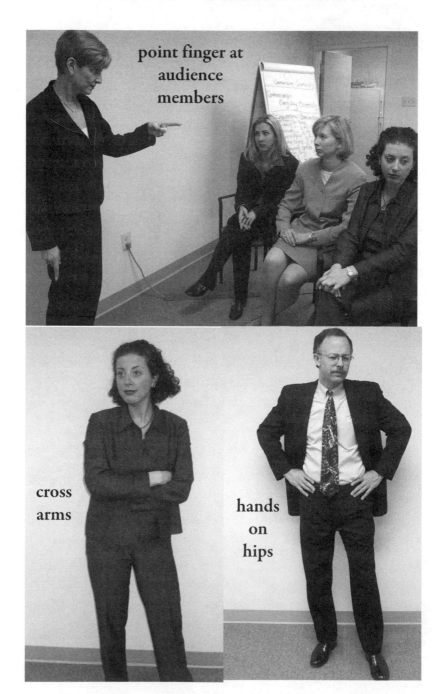

point finger at audience members

cross arms

hands on hips

Gestures also help you to emphasize important points during your presentation. They reinforce what you are saying with a visual message. The most effective gestures are spontaneous ones. They come from what you are thinking and feeling, and help the audience members relate to you and what you are telling them. It is much more effective to watch a speaker who uses movement, than to listen to someone standing behind a lectern with hands clasped in front of him or her.

You can use gestures effectively

Have you ever watched an evangelist on television using wide, sweeping gestures while speaking? These gestures are effective, because they include everyone, making viewers feel a part of things even though they are watching from their own home. As a presenter in a business setting, you will be using gestures sparingly, and only to emphasize points in your presentation.

But like the TV evangelist, when you gesture, use the upper quadrant of your body, and make your gestures up and out to the audience. Your movements should be broad and flowing, not fast and jerky. The most effective gestures are natural extensions of yourself.

Vary your gestures; don't use the same motion over and over again. Repetition can be distracting to audience members, and you may find they are watching your gestures instead of listening to the presentation. Some gestures interfere with the audience's ability to pay attention, such as the threatening ones mentioned ear-

Seated Position -- What to Do

open gestures

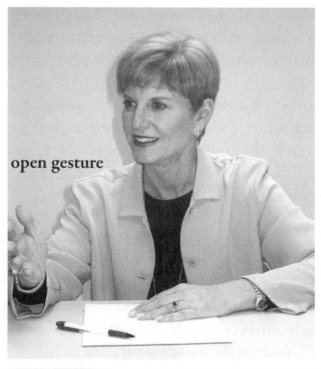

open gesture

Gestures -- What to Do

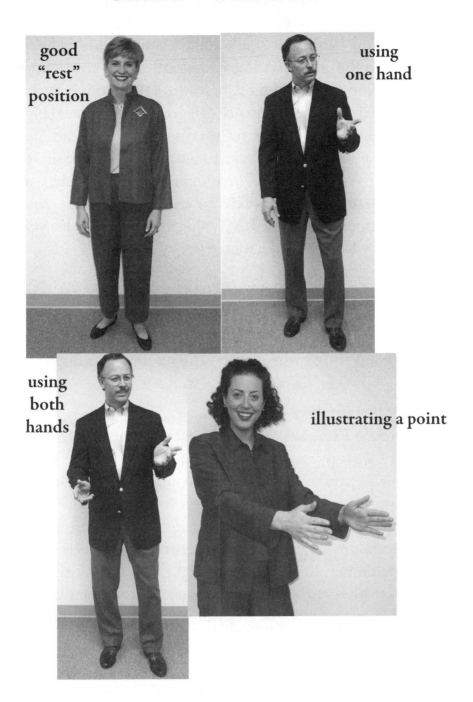

good "rest" position

using one hand

using both hands

illustrating a point

lier (finger pointing and fist waving). Instead, use your palms and open them out to your audience. Move your arm and hand as a single unit, gesturing up and out toward the audience. Use either one or two arms. Try a sweeping motion and relate the extent of your gestures to the size of your audience. Bigger audiences need bigger gestures. Don't forget that nodding the head and smiling are effective ways to emphasize what you are saying. As a presenter who uses gestures effectively, you will be projecting confidence and competence – and the response you get from your audience will let you know when you have succeeded.

Listeners feel more comfortable with a speaker who gestures effectively. Gestures work best when they are natural and spontaneous. Practiced gestures can look stiff and stilted when used during a presentation. You can, however, learn how to gesture effectively.

Practice Exercise: Stand in front of a full-length mirror. Get into a comfortable stance. How does it look? Now, separate your feet approximately 6 to 8 inches apart. Drop your arms loosely to your sides. Now practice a variety of gestures. What feels uncomfortable (because it is new) may look terrific. What feels comfortable may look sloppy or tight. Do these exercises three times a week for one minute. Within a month or two, your natural gestures will be more open and fluid.

Keys to effective gesturing

- Use gestures to emphasize major points.
- Let your movements be broad and flowing, not fast and jerky.
- Vary your gestures.
- Don't point your finger or fist -- these gestures can be intimidating.
- Use your palms and open them to your audience.
- Move your arm and hand together as a single unit to avoid floppy wrists or elbows.
- Use large gestures for a large audience and narrow them for a smaller group.
- Evaluate your gestures by doing them in front of a mirror.
- Avoid gestures that make you seem nervous or defensive.
- Don't stand with your hands behind your back or crossed in front of you.
- Don't keep your hands in your pockets.
- Keep hands and gestures above your waist.
- Gestures should be upward and open.
- Nods and smiles will make you seem confident to your audience.

The Vocal

Your voice plays a big part of audience perception. When we are stressed, our voices tend to rise, but the deeper the pitch, the longer people will listen to what you have to say. You can learn to gain control over your pitch and bring it into a lower range. Try this exercise.

Repeat the following three sentences, each time using a deeper pitch: "This is my normal pitch." "Do, Re, Me, Fa, So, La, Ti, Do." "This is my normal voice."

Stop and listen for differences between the first and last sentences. Repeat the trio of sentences until you are in control of your pitch, and can deepen it at will. Practice this exercise 10 times each day, and after six weeks you will have greater control over your pitch.

Volume

Even the most interesting presentation will fail if it can't be heard; conversely, if it is delivered in a very loud voice, it will fail as well – since people will feel that you are shouting at them. Being able to control your volume, and vary it, will help you hold the audience's attention.

To help you control your volume, try this exercise: Breathe from the diaphragm, and speak as if your voice is hitting the back wall of the room you are in. Breathing from the diaphragm allows more air flow, and will help to avoid a sore throat when projecting.

Fast talk/slow talk

The normal speaking rate is between 120 and 160 words per minute. If people are always asking you to repeat yourself, you probably talk too fast. If they are usually interrupting you, you probably speak too slowly. To control your rate, read aloud. Take 120, 140 or 160 words from a book or magazine, and time yourself as you read them. Based on the results, you will know whether to slow down or speed up your normal rate. Practice every day until comfortable with your new rate of speech. Rate may need to be varied, depending on your audience. Southern audiences may use a slower rate than many Northern audiences. When English isn't a first language, the speaker will need to speak more slowly. If the information is very technical, the speaker will need to slow down and pause frequently for the audience to assess the meaning.

Diction

Many mispronunciation problems are the result of bad diction habits and regional peculiarities. In some areas of the country, it is common to hear the endings of words clipped off or changed, for example: gonna for going, doin for doing, thinkin for thinking, em for them. Most pronunciation and diction problems can be corrected by listening to good speakers, asking when you are not sure how to pronounce a word, looking unfamiliar words up in the dictionary or by coaching from a qualified speech instructor.

Emphasis

When we speak, we tend to emphasize certain words or phrases. In your presentations, the words and phrases you emphasize should be ones that will bring home your point to the audience. You can change the meaning of a sentence simply by changing position of the words you emphasize. The technique used to emphasize words or phrases in your presentation is called "punching" it. Professional speakers and speech writers underline the words and phrases they want to emphasize. You can do the same on your own outline and when you practice the presentation, practice "punching" it as well. For example, in this sentence, the emphasis changes the speaker's intent: "When we deal with companies *your* size ..." compared to "When we deal with companies your *size* ... ."

Pause to punctuate

The pause is as critical in oral language as punctuation is to written language. When you fill pauses with "and," "uh," and "um," it is not only distracting, but also doesn't allow the audience members to think about what you are saying. In your mind, when you get to a period, count to three; a colon, count to two; and a comma, count to one. Don't rush your ideas or sound hesitant by using fillers.

Pauses are also frequently misused. An effective pause emphasizes what has just been said, or what is to come. For example, if you are going to announce a decision you have made, or a new product your company is coming out with, your speech should have pauses for dramatic emphasis. "Our company has developed a way to remove the fat content from foods. This new product, now available in test markets, will change the way the world eats (pause) -- we call it 'Remove.'" This brief pause sets audience members up to hear the announcement of a new product called "Remove."

Even if they were only half listening before, when the speaker pauses, he or she recaptures their attention. They want to know what's coming after the pause. On the other hand, there are some pauses that can hurt your presentation -- pauses that detract from what you are trying to say because they come at inappropriate times during your presentation -- often when you have forgotten what you wanted to say or lost your place.

Voice problems

Your voice becomes a problem when it calls attention to itself. There are several common voice problems:

- Harshness – unless it is physical in nature, a harsh voice indicates tension and stress. Use relaxation techniques to help eliminate the problem. If your throat is dry, drink warm water with lemon before speaking.
- Nasality – frequently caused by clenched jaws, it can be reduced by opening the mouth wider and using the tongue more firmly.
- Breathlessness – usually caused by insufficient breathing while speaking. Take deeper breaths and release a controlled flow of air.
- High pitch – unless physical in nature, can be improved with vocal exercises and a conscious effort to speak in your lower vocal range.

Finish with strength

Does your voice tend to rise at the end of a sentence?

Record yourself speaking the first few lines of your presentation. If your voice goes up at the end of a sentence, it will sound as though you are asking a question or are tentative about what you just said. If you tend to swallow your last few words, that will reduce the impact of what you are saying as well. Finish sentences completely, and drop your pitch slightly while keeping the volume strong. Listen to newscasters as they close their broadcasts; most of them use a tag line which they repeat regularly with volume up and pitch down. Practice until comfortable with the way you sound.

The Verbal

What you have to say is important, and communicating your ideas clearly and concisely will be the greatest challenge as a presenter. Your audience members will be looking for "WIIFM" (What's In It For Me?) from the moment you begin to speak. Make sure your opening tells them what they can expect to get from your presentation. One key to audience acceptance and respect is to talk the way your audience does. It means you should keep the audience in mind when writing your presentation, so you can use familiar words and concepts that will be of interest. Avoid jargon and acronyms, and define technical language.

Consider using anecdotes to bring yourself into the world of your listeners by relating experiences you may have in common with them. If your presentation is to a technical group, by all means use technical terms and jargon, but also using some colorful language could make your presentation even more interesting. For all presentations, use simple, descriptive language. Adjust your vocabulary to suit the group. The more you know about who comprises your audience, the easier it will be for you to speak their language. Avoid using foreign phrases, unless you are planning on translating them for the audience. Keep your sentences and words short. What words can you eliminate to make your speech more concise? If you are using language that can mean different things to different members of the audience, be sure to explain your meaning. For example, "politics" can refer to a system or government, or refer to the inner dynamics of an organization.

There is a world of difference between mentioning that a product is "cheap" and saying it is "inexpensive." Be sure you have taken the audience's industry or profession in mind when preparing your presentation. Be sincere and don't ever pretend that you have things in common with your audience when you don't. Be honest. Your words will paint a picture for your listeners, and using colorful and descriptive language will help you bring it to life for them.

Power robbers & tag questions

We hear competent speakers every day. Listen to radio or television and you will hear confident, authoritative men and women telling us about the news, current events, or even endorsing products. How do these people sound, and what kind of words do they use? The professional speakers in our world use clear, colorful language in short, simple sentences that are easy to understand.

Many of us, however, hem and haw, trying to find the right word, or use filler words. We may even discount ourselves and our ideas without realizing it.

All of these verbal faults are "Power Robbers" that detract from our confidence, authority, professionalism and power. Hedges and qualifiers are also common power robbers. These are the filler words we use when we are uncertain about what we have to say or are uncomfortable with silence. Examples are: "I guess," "I hope," "probably," "kinda," "sorta" and "maybe." "Um," "ah," "like" and "you know" are also distracting and annoying if they are abundant.

I recently went to hear a psychologist speak. She had an interesting topic and was a very attractive presenter. Unfortunately, she had a very annoying habit that detracted from her presentation. After the first five minutes, I found myself counting the "ums" in her speech just out of curiosity. I stopped counting at 100.

Passive sentences are also power robbers. Active sentences show we took the initiative and performed an action. Passive sentences and words say that things happened to us or around us. For example: "I hit the ball" (active), or, "The ball was hit by me" (passive).

Active words give us more power. For example: "Due to the increased client demand, I was forced to develop my organizational and writing skills." A more powerful, active way to say this is: "I developed my organizational skills and sharpened my professional writing abilities to better service growing client demands." This demonstrates your initiative and effort in the situation in a positive way.

Two of the most powerful words in the English language are "you" and "I." The word "you" is most effective when influencing, persuading, or selling to someone. The focus should be on the person we are speaking to. After all, he or she is not going to do something just because we think it's a good idea. The person is going to respond to what he or she thinks, feels and wants. Most of our statements in business should be you-based. "This is a great new copy machine. Imagine all the benefits to you and your company." The word "I" is best used in a conflict situation. When we are in conflict, we often begin by accusing and attacking the other person. "You were wrong. You made a mistake. You made me look bad." The other person, upon hearing this tirade of you's, begins to withdraw or becomes defensive. Either way, the communication is stopped because the person is no longer listening. A more effective way to approach conflicts is to use the word "I." "I feel that there was a mistake made. I was embarrassed and felt we could have been better prepared." Nothing in that statement is directly accusing, yet you are still getting your message across and chances are the other person is still listening.

Three strong words to use are "urge," "recommend," and "suggest." The idea behind understanding which words send certain messages, is to make conscious decisions about the words we choose. Instead of saying things out of habit, be aware of what you say and create new, more effective habits when you speak.

Tag questions

Tag questions can cut your effectiveness. These are questions at the end of a sentence that give the impression you are unsure of what was just said, or are looking for approval. "I know my group's solution to fighting the rumors is a good one, isn't it?" The "isn't it?" gives that strong, declarative sentence a weak ending. Think about what you really want to say, and how you are going to say it. Then say exactly what you mean.

You can work to minimize the effect of power robbers on your speaking habits in three ways:

- by identifying your own tendencies
- by correcting the behavior
- by practicing to permanently replace the bad habit with a good one

The way you pronounce words also can undermine your ability to influence people. Even the best prepared, researched, written, and practiced presentation will fail if you mispronounce words or use them incorrectly. People who mispronounce words are thought to be poorly educated or not very bright. This is frequently untrue. If you are unsure about a pronunciation, look it up in the dictionary.

Words to avoid:

- Slang
- Foul language
- Undefined acronyms, jargon and buzz words
- Pretentious language
- Power robbers
- "To tell you the truth," "To be perfectly honest" – Be honest and truthful ... no need to say it!

Remember the three V's

Visual:
- Dress appropriately to help, not hinder your presentation.
- Step out from behind the lectern, or better yet, don't use one at all.
- Smile when appropriate.
- Get set before starting to speak.
- Establish eye contact with audience members.
- Begin speaking without looking at your notes.
- Refer to your outline only occasionally.
- Don't look at the floor or out the window.
- Use gestures effectively (open palms, vary motions; keep them visible, smooth, natural).
- Stand up straight yet relaxed; don't lean.
- Use facial expressions to add interest, look confident.

- Keep your chin up.
- Keep your feet still (no dancing, shifting or crossing legs). Keep your movements intentional.
- Don't pace.
- Move about, leave the podium. Get closer to the audience.
- Look like you are enjoying yourself.
- Seem to care that your audience listens ... better yet, care.
- Appear confident and relaxed.
- Don't play with pens, pointers, visuals, hair, jewelry, or rattle change in your pocket.
- Don't pack up to leave before the audience has left.

Vocal:
- Speak with enthusiasm.
- Be interested and sincere.
- Be spontaneous, not like you are reading or have memorized your presentation.
- Keep your pitch comfortable and low; use variation in tone.
- Keep your speaking rate at 125-160 words per minute. Vary the rate. Not too fast, not too slow.
- Pronounce your words carefully. Enunciate clearly.
- Use pauses for impact.
- Use voice variation (pitch, volume, rate, punch).
- Stop at the end of an idea; don't hook sentences together with "and," "and uh," or "like."
- Drop your pitch, not volume, at the end of sentences; and don't let your voice rise at the end of declarative statements.
- Hide, don't emphasize your mistakes.

Verbal:

- Use descriptive language.
- Start with a grabber to get their interest and create need.
- Use transitions to make your ideas flow.
- Use short sentences.
- Write for the ear, not the eye.
- Avoid power robbers.
- Make sure your information is interesting, useful, and understandable.
- Repeat the information to enhance retention.
- Avoid words that create doubt about what you are saying ("kind of," "sort of," "I hope," "I guess," "perhaps").
- Speak with, not at, the audience.

For that perfect delivery ...

1. Turn off any visuals that have been showing to focus the audience's attention solely on you. Breathe deeply, take the platform, face the audience, make eye contact, and proceed with the introduction, grabber first. Movement begins only after the opening is finished.

2. Prepare for interruptions. Many interruptions can be avoided by taking simple precautions ahead of time.

- Close the doors to the presentation room.
- Post a sign that warns a presentation is in progress.
- Have an associate posted by the door to stop interruptions, when appropriate.
- Re-route or turn off any phones in the room.
- Encourage your audience members to put cell

phones and pagers on vibrate mode.
- Tell audience members when they can ask questions.
- Let the audience know when any breaks will be.

3. Avoid getting off track. There is always potential danger when departing from the planned outline, and addressing subjects originally not intended as part of the presentation. Whether precipitated by an audience member's question or the speaker's desire to be as informative as possible, the result is often a loss of focus and, with it, a reduction in the presentation's effectiveness. Getting off track can often be avoided by an awareness of the danger ahead of time, and a conscious effort to avoid it. This effort should be one of the motivating factors in the development of a tight outline, and a final draft that can be easily referred to during the presentation.

Speaking without notes should only be considered if there has been sufficient rehearsal to have the outline thoroughly learned. If, despite precautions, the presentation gets off track, use your notes to determine what was last covered, and then resume. If a question is asked that will take you off track, agree to discuss it later. If the question is asked by a client or manager, answer it briefly, then get back on track.

4. If questions have followed the presentation, a second closing is needed. A lackluster ending, often consisting of a mumbled reference to the lack of more questions or time, should be avoided at all costs. You now have another opportunity to reinforce your main points and make a memorable statement.

5. Get feedback from both audience members and unbiased sources to help you to improve your presentation skills. When appropriate, evaluation forms can be distributed; when not, follow-up calls to audience members can be helpful. Unobtrusive tape recorders and video cameras can be particularly helpful by showing the speaker what the audience experienced.

Practice Techniques
- Practice out loud, three to six times.
- Say the presentation differently each time to keep the spontaneity.
- Practice where you will be speaking, if possible, or simulate the environment.
- Practice using your visual aids.
- Tape record your practice. Listen, then make changes.
- Videotape your presentation, watch it, make any necessary adjustments in content and delivery.
- Practice in front of someone similar to your audience.

Part Nine

Questions & Answers

"I'm about winning."
-- **"Magic" Johnson,** played on many championship
L.A. Lakers teams

The end of your presentation does not come when you finish speaking. After your conclusion, you still have another opportunity to face your audience members and leave them with a final positive impression.

The question-and-answer period will have an impact on your audience. Do not try to escape this crucial time by sitting down or leaving the podium. This is an opportunity for you to further clarify your ideas. You don't want to give the audience the impression that you are relieved that your presentation is over, and all you want to do is leave. These simple rules will guide you through the process for a successful question-and-answer period.

• Early in your presentation, preferably as part of the preview, tell audience members when you will be taking questions; you may ask them to write them down to save for the end; to ask throughout your presentation, or at specific breaking points during the presentation, whichever works best for you, and meets audience objectives and time allotments.

- Before answering questions, listen carefully and paraphrase the question – or include the question as part of your answer before you respond.
- Look at the questioner while paraphrasing or include the question as part of the answer, but look at the entire audience when answering.
- Call on experts in the audience when appropriate, but take back control after they have responded.
- Control hostile questioners.
- Tell those with multiple questions that aren't relevant to the entire group that you will respond either at the end of the session or later to them in writing or by telephone.
- Don't let a stage hog take control.
- Don't tell a lie. If you don't know the answer to a question, say so and offer to get the information for the questioner – or tell the person where he or she can get it.
- End the question-and-answer period with a strong closing remark.

How to encourage questions

It is part of your job as a presenter to encourage questions from the audience. Open up by asking, "What questions do you have?" or "Who would like to ask the first question?" Be sure to wait up to 10 seconds before commenting. You must give people time to think about the question they may want to ask. In some groups, no one will raise a hand and go first, so you will have to make the first move. You can do this by saying, "A question I am usually asked is ... ." That should encourage others to speak up after you have answered your own question.

Your position during this period should be closer to the audience. Step out from behind your lectern or table, even sit at the side of the conference table if the audience will still be able to see you. Some speakers like to take questions while they stand amidst the audience. If the room setup is appropriate and you feel comfortable, it is acceptable to run the question-and-answer period this way.

Pay close attention to your own body language, keeping it open and favorable. Avoid rolling your eyes, sighing or cleaning up your notes. If people are not asking questions, it probably means they are bored, confused, afraid to look or sound stupid, they did not like your presentation or want to leave. If after the first question no one else volunteers one, it is appropriate to wrap up your presentation with some final words. This can be another conclusion, you can return to your central theme, revert to your closing statement, or talk about next steps. Keep your remarks brief, and end with a strong finish.

How to control questions

As the presenter, it is up to you to control the question-and-answer period. Your first decision is when you want to answer questions. If you are giving a training session or a sales presentation, it probably makes sense to take questions during your presentation. Don't get too far ahead of yourself. If someone asks a question that you will be covering later in your presentation, tell the person that. You must also avoid a lengthy response to a question which may disturb your train of thought and the audience's ability to concentrate. You can also set aside question-and-answer periods at specified times during a presentation and announce them at the start of your program. This gives your audience members the chance to formulate their questions during your presentation. You can also ask the audience to wait until the end before asking.

How to handle hostility

As a presenter, you may find yourself facing a hostile questioner. Your skill at disarming verbal attacks will reflect on your credibility with audience members and the impression they have of you and your presentation. By remembering the acronym **VIPP**, you can diffuse hostile questioners:

V – Let them say whatever they want. You listen while they **Vent**.

I – Use an "**I**" statement to show empathy by paraphrasing what they have just said, and how they feel about it -- but don't be condescending.

P – Ask **Probing** questions to try to find out what the real issues are.

P – Choose one of the following statements or a variation to **Problem** solve: "I know what your issues are, now let me respond." "Let's problem solve together to work this out." "Let's look into this after this presentation has concluded."

By using the **VIPP** approach, you have indicated that you value the questioner's thoughts and feelings. The audience will respect you, and you will diffuse the hostility at the same time.

Above all, don't allow yourself to engage in an argument with an audience member. Always look to diffuse a situation, rather than allow it to escalate. Other techniques to use include:

- Leave your "but" out of an argument. "Yes. That happened, and (not but) look at what we are doing about it."
- When someone says, "Your information isn't correct," respond: "Where did your information come from?" Or, if the person says: "I don't agree," respond, "What about it don't you agree with?" You can always do what politicians do – spin your answer: "What you really want to be asking ..."

How to respond to questions

When you know the answer: A good way to begin when

you know the answer, is to paraphrase the question or include it as part of the answer. This clarifies the fact that you understand the question, and have heard it correctly – and ensures that the rest of the audience members hear the question. Then answer it. Avoid the tendency to say, "That's a good question" before you answer, or "As I said in my presentation," or "Did I answer your question?" after you have responded.

When you compliment one questioner, it becomes awkward if you don't compliment the next questioner, and so on. If you have asked, "Did I answer your question?" and the answer is negative, you have destroyed some of your credibility with the audience. You also run the risk of embarrassing the questioner if he or she doesn't understand your answer. A good way to make sure you have answered the question is to ask the same questioner if he or she has any other questions for you, or whether more explanation would be helpful. When you do know the answer, keep your answer short and interesting to most of the group (long answers discourage more questions). If the question isn't relevant to most people, tell the questioner that you will meet with him or her after the presentation. If the decision maker is asking the question, take the time to answer it.

When you don't know the answer to a question, be truthful. Simply say, "I don't have the answer," or "I don't have that information," and you can offer to get the information and get back to that person at a later time. Ask the person to give you his card with the question on it, or write it down yourself with the person's phone number. You also can offer the person a source for the information, or you can open it up to the audience or an expert in the group who may know the answer. Don't dwell on it, keep the question-and-answer session moving. Do anticipate the questions in advance and prepare answers. Don't make up answers.

If you encounter a *stage hog* who asks you one question after another, you will need to make a decision. If the questions are relevant and merit consideration, answer them. But after answering a few, nicely say it's time to give someone else a turn. If the questions are not relevant, answer the first question or two and then cut him or her short. If you have identified a potential stage hog prior to your presentation, try meeting with the person in advance to discuss any ideas. Mention any that have merit during your presentation; that will make him or her feel good and probably save you from disruption of your question-and-answer period.

Ending with a strong finish:

When your presentation is over, and the questions have stopped, or time is up, it's time to conclude. Don't make the mistake of saying "thank you" and leaving the podium. This is your last chance to leave a positive impression. Return to the central theme, revert to your closing statement, or talk about next steps. Your closing should not be lengthy, but wrap things up neatly. An example might be: "We've learned how and why

Vest-A-Cop programs work, now it is up to us to make our police officers and our citizens safer."

Final thoughts on questions & answers

- Tell audience members when you will take questions, and if there is a time limit on the number they can ask.
- Encourage questions by having an open body stance and personal enthusiasm.
- Ask a question yourself, if necessary.
- Listen carefully and paraphrase before responding.
- Look at the questioner when paraphrasing a question, look at the audience when responding.
- If you don't know the answer, say so. Offer to get back to the person in writing or by phone.
- Don't let a stage hog take control.
- Handle hostile questioners with tact and diplomacy, but cut them short.
- Respect the questioner and don't be defensive.
- Keep your answers brief.
- End the question-and-answer session with a memorable closing

Part Ten

Special Types of Presentations

"When you go to the Olympic Games, you're taking the rest of the world, in front of the entire world."
-- **Bruce Jenner,** Olympic gold medalist

Many of the opportunities you will have to make presentations throughout your career will involve other speakers. These occasions may take the form of panel discussions, symposiums, forums, and other group situations. To be effective, team presentations must be meticulously planned and executed and well coordinated like a ballet where each dancer knows exactly where to stand, when to move, and when to exit from the stage.

The stakes are often high, as in the award of advertising contracts where millions of dollars ride on the presentation dynamics of one advertising agency team vs. a team from another agency – often with the same levels of experience and creativity. What makes one team stand out? If the team works like a smooth, well-oiled machine, if one member's presentation flows into the next presentation, and if all members present themselves professionally and intelligently, the impression left is one of confidence and competence. Team presentations come with their own unique set of problems. For a single presenter, developing a well-crafted and executed presentation falls on his or her shoulders alone. But as part of a group, there is the added constraint of worrying about the rest of the team. Decisions have to be made in concert with the other team members, and this can lead to confusion and controversy. It is, therefore, essential to have one strong team leader who will guide and coordinate members' presentations, making sure each person has his or her area covered adequately, and ensuring that one member's presentation does not duplicate someone else's.

Six steps to a successful team presentation

1. Pick the right leader. Often the person with seniority is automatically designated team leader. This may not work if that person is busy with other projects or has too much day-to-day responsibility to spend the time necessary coordinating all members' presentations. The team leader should be the person with the most knowledge of the topic or the client, one who the other members respect and someone they know is objective and will give them fair criticism.

2. Agreement on the focus. Each member of a team should be aware that his or her contribution is essential to the overall success, and no one member's part is more important than another's.

3. Frequent updates and review of material. All team members should be discussing their part of the presentation with the team leader to ensure they are headed in the right direction. Group meetings should be held so everyone is aware of where the other members are heading.

4. Proper audience analysis. Team presentations are usually given to other teams. This means the audience members may come from different levels in their organization, from different departments, and have different agendas of their own. Each member of the presenting team should understand who the audience is, and consider its knowledge levels and interests.

5. Pay attention to details. The leader or a designate should have responsibility for the details such as room arrangements, equipment, visual aids, and handouts. Everything in a team presentation should be coordinated and reviewed well in advance of presentation day. This person should also arrange for the team members to practice in the room where they will be presenting, if possible.

6. Mutual respect for team members. The group dynamics will be apparent to the audience. A team that works well together, respects each other's part in the presentation, and enjoys being together will have the advantage. If your team is made up of people from different departments who may not have had the chance to meet, schedule an informal lunch or dinner so they can have the chance to get to know each other. The comfort level the team members have with each other will help them to relax and do their best during the presentation.

If you are the team leader

If you are the team leader, much of the planning and details will be your responsibility. The other members of the team will be looking to you for guidance and validation that their presentations will be effective. To ensure the best for your team, your responsibilities should include the following:

- Buy-in of the concepts and strategies from management. It is up to you to schedule a meeting with key people before the team begins working. This will avoid having to do things over again later if management doesn't agree with the direction you have taken. The support of management will be important to team members, and will help to encourage them.
- Audience analysis. As team leader, you should be prepared to gather information on the audience. If other members of the team have more contact with the audience, assign them the job of preparing the audience analysis. This information should include the key players and decision makers in the audience.
- Define the strategy for your team. You have met with management and mapped out a strategy for the presentation. It is up to you to meet with your team, and make sure each member is comfortable with the strategy. It is also up to you to give a

clear picture of the audience and marketing strategy to those members of the team who may lack insight into these areas.

- Assign the topics as sections of the presentation. If you have chosen your team or had them assigned to you, as leader you will most likely be assigning each presenter his or her topic. In creative presentations, writers and art directors know what their areas are, but it is still up to the leader to explain what each member of the team is expected to do.
- Make a schedule. You should schedule time for individual meetings with each presenter, and for the group to meet for run-throughs and updates. This will give team members the chance to familiarize themselves with each other's work, and to see how the presentation fits together.
- Provide strong leadership and direction. The team members will be looking to you to make sure everything is on track. It is up to you to stay on schedule, on budget, and on course. Failing to provide strong leadership may result in missed deadlines, extensive rework and an unhappy team. This will lead to poor performance.

If you are the moderator of a panel discussion

- It is your responsibility to introduce the topic to be discussed and each speaker. It should have been decided beforehand if the moderator will list the panelists' credentials, or if each panelist will give a brief self-introduction.

- You will be opening and closing each segment of the discussion. It will also be your responsibility to maintain proper timing to give each panelist a fair time share. The moderator keeps track of how long each speaker has to make his or her point, and warns when time is running out. If the speaker keeps going over the allotted time, it is up to the moderator to stop the presentation.
- The moderator will also provide a bridge between speech segments, and may or may not comment between presenters. He or she may simply move the discussion along if comments are not appropriate.

The moderator opens the question-and-answer session, paraphrases the questions and calls on the person who will respond. At the end of the question-and-answer period, it is the moderator's responsibility to end the discussion and conclude.

Meetings that work

Many of the presentations you will give throughout your business career will be at meetings. On average, executives spend more than 50 percent of their time at meetings. Whether or not that time is well spent is the question. If you are the person calling the meeting, be sure to ask yourself the question, "Is a meeting really necessary?" before you schedule one. Clearly understanding the objectives will help you to determine if a meeting is needed. What is your desired end result? Is there an alternative to a meeting that will be just as effective? What are the alternatives? Once your objectives are known, it becomes easier to decide the best way to achieve them. A meeting may be the only answer, but phone calls, e-mail, or memos might be just as effective.

If you are asked by someone else to arrange a meeting, your first task is to answer the question, "What is the purpose?" It may be:

- To solve a problem
- To share information
- To plan a strategy
- To gather information
- To provide instruction
- To showcase someone's abilities
- To brainstorm ideas
- To review data

When a meeting is planned without thought to its purpose, the attendees often arrive with competing or conflicting perceptions of why they are there. It is advised that an agenda or memo defining the purpose of the meeting be distributed to all invitees prior to scheduling the meeting. This way, if there is another way to accomplish the purpose, or an alternative method of dealing with it, you will find out in advance.

If a meeting is needed, who should attend? The purpose of the meeting should determine who needs to be there.

In large corporations, representatives from various divisions may be needed; in a small organization, only a decision maker and one or two others may be sufficient. In selecting who to invite to the meeting, your objectives as a presenter should be considered. If you are not the organizer, but have been asked to present, there may be someone in the organization you want to hear your presentation – either because it affects him or her directly, or because you want this person to see you in action. Request that he or she be invited, and let the organizer know why.

Successful meetings require careful planning. If you will be creating the agenda, how should you present the information? Agendas should be brief and to the point. You could use phrasing in the form of questions, accompanied by a brief statement of justification for including the item on the agenda. If the agenda is covering only one topic and various participants will be presenting segments, use the purpose as the title of the meeting and include each participant's segment, name, department, and title. It also is important to include a timetable.

When scheduling a meeting, it is your responsibility to make sure the basic requirements for the room are arranged.

- Is the room large enough for the number of attendees?
- Is there adequate light and air?
- Is the room isolated from outside interruptions?
- Is the room convenient for attendees?
- Is the room available for the time you have scheduled?
- Is there adequate seating?

- If you will be using audio/visual/computer equipment, will it be supplied and is the room properly wired?
- Use the following worksheet to help you.

Meeting planning worksheet

1. Objectives: What are the desired results of this meeting?

2. Time: How long will it last? When should it be held?

3. Attendees: Who needs to be there? Are decision makers, information presenters and information gatherers included?

4. Agenda: What is the schedule of events? Who is involved in preparing and distributing the agenda?

5. Physical Arrangements: What kind of facilities and equipment are needed? What are the specific room arrangements?

6. Evaluations: How will the meeting be evaluated?

Meeting Agenda

AGENDA

Meeting Title: Meetings That Get Results

Meeting Location: *to be determined*

Participants: *to be determined*

Meeting Leader: *to be determined*

Date: *to be determined*

Start Time: *to be determined*

End Time: *to be determined*

Breaks: *to be determined*

Please Bring: Specific learning objectives, your experiences with meetings, an open mind, ideas to share, pens, and paper.

Special Notes: Everyone arrives on time, participates and has fun, and leaves with specific action items to apply.

AGENDA	PERSONS RESPONSIBLE	TIME ALLOTTED
• Introduction and Objectives	• Facilitator	• 60 minutes
• Planning a meeting	• Facilitator and Participants	• 120 minutes
• Lunch	• All	• 60 minutes
• Facilitating a meeting	• Facilitator and Participants	• 90 minutes
• Decision Making	• Facilitator and Participants	• 30 minutes
• Practice Session	• Participants	• 90 minutes
• Conclusion	• Facilitator	• 15 minutes

During the meeting planning stage, you will need to prepare an agenda. Prior to issuing the actual agenda, survey the proposed participants to find out their needs and concerns so that the final agenda is planned with those needs in mind. This is also a way to surface hidden agendas. A brief memo may be distributed to accomplish this, and can include the following three questions:

1. What topics would you like to present during our meeting on _____?
2. How much time will you need to present?
3. What issues or concerns would you like to be discussed?

You will then be able to plan and distribute your agenda prior to the meeting. On the day of the meeting, bring enough agendas along to distribute to participants along with any background materials, charts, markers, pads, pens, flip charts, etc., that may not be supplied for you. If you will be leading the meeting, you will have 10 basic responsibilities:

1. Start the meeting promptly.
2. State the objectives and ground rules. (Ask people to turn off cell phones and PDAs).
3. Follow the agenda.
4. Manage the flow.
5. Facilitate discussion.
6. Deal with problems/difficult participants.
7. Help to resolve conflicts.
8. Clarify next steps/action plan.
9. Summarize.
10. Evaluate.

As a meeting leader, you may be faced with handling difficult participants. These usually fall into one or more of five categories: overly dominating; rambling; side conversationalists; non-contributors and negative participants. Here are some suggestions for dealing with these problems:

Overly dominating: Credit the speaker's knowledge of the subject and any constructive contributions. State the need for others to be heard. Ask the group for reactions. Intervene in personal attacks by partially paraphrasing informational content of the attack, if there is any. If the participant is out of line, acknowledge his or her feelings and move on.

Rambling: Wait for a break or pause and intervene. Confirm your understanding of the basic points. Restate the urgency of time constraints. Direct a question to another participant or the group, and refocus or restate the objectives.

Side conversationalists: Stop speaking and look at the talkers. Ask them if they have any questions. Restate objectives, and ask them to hold side conversations until the meeting has ended. Lower your volume and move toward them. Avoid embarrassing people.

Non-contributors: You don't want to embarrass them, but you could try to involve them through direct questions. Talk to non-contributors at break time to find out why they are quiet. Give them specific responsibilities.

Negative participants: Find out if the negative feelings are shared by the group. Ask the negative person to record the minutes; this keeps him or her busy and less able to speak out. Talk to this person individually at break time to try to uncover the reason for the negativity.

Evaluating the meeting

Meetings should be evaluated in two ways: by the meeting leader, and by the participants. In small, informal meetings, an evaluation can take place at the close of the meeting during the summation or final remarks of the meeting leader. For larger meetings, the following personal evaluation forms can help you to clarify whether the meeting met its objectives and get the participants' feelings.

Personal evaluation for meeting leaders

- Was this meeting necessary?
- Were my objectives clear?
- Was my agenda organized and distributed before the meeting?
- Did I invite only/all necessary participants?
- Did I arrive early, and check on the room arrangements and the equipment?
- Did the meeting begin/end on time?
- Was the agenda followed?
- Did I stay within allotted time frames?

- Did I encourage participation?
- Did I effectively resolve conflicts?
- Did I maintain control?
- Were the final decisions summarized and action plan outlined?
- Did I follow up by sending minutes to participants?
- Was there an evaluation?
- Was follow-up action done by the participants?

Personal evaluation for meeting participants

- Was the purpose of the meeting clear to me?
- Did I understand my role?
- Did I prepare my information well?
- Was I on time?
- Did I conduct side conversations during the meeting?
- Did I ask pertinent/relevant questions?
- Was I open to the ideas of others?
- Was I a good listener?
- Did I participate as fully as possible?
- Did I help to facilitate/maintain discussion?
- Did I complete the follow-up action?
- Did I evaluate the meeting and give helpful feedback?

Closing the meeting

The meeting leader should be the one who ends the meeting. It is best to give a five- or 10-minute warning, giving group members time to finish their remarks. If the meeting has fallen behind and some items on the agenda cannot be completed, the leader must indicate these and propose an alternative time or method for including them. As leader, your responsibilities also include:

Summarizing the conclusions and stating:

- how the meeting was useful
- the objectives that were achieved
- the next steps to be taken
- areas of responsibility

Thanking the group by:

- expressing appreciation for everyone's participation
- giving credit to individuals

If an additional meeting of the same group has been scheduled, the leader should include this in the closing remarks.

Videoconferences

While telephones, e-mail, and the written word are still the primary methods of business communication, the "information age" and video have taken us much farther in our ability to communicate face-to-face. It is so much better to see the person we are dealing with, whether that person is across town or on the other side of the globe. With videoconferencing joining other mainstream methods of communication, we can be face-to-face with anyone, anywhere in the world. Many corporations have their own videoconferencing facilities, with in-house staff to make things work smoothly. But you don't have to work for a large corporation to take advantage of videoconferencing. Many rental facilities exist, staffed by experts who can guide you step-by-step through the process.

The capability to link two or more locations almost anywhere in the world makes videoconferencing valuable for companies doing business globally. Giving a presentation over a videoconferencing network is very different from presenting to a live audience.

Imagine yourself projected onto the screen of your computer. How will you look and sound? You will probably be seated, facing a camera, and a video screen will show people on the other end of the conference. They will be in a similar setup. You will probably appear primarily as a talking head. Your visual aids will be presented through another camera, leading to confusion if you have not carefully choreographed with the camera operator when to show them. Find out in advance if you will be able to stand or show the visuals yourself. When preparing your presentation, keep the camera setup in mind. If you are unsure of how to prepare, meet in advance with the program facilitator, who may be able to show you a sample of an actual videoconference or demonstrate how it will work.

Tips for videoconferences

- **Size counts:** Videoconferences are best suited to small, geographically dispersed groups. With large groups it is difficult to see other participants.

- **Have a backup plan if things malfunction.** Consider an audio conference or Webinar if the video fails.

- **Make proper introductions.** Once connected, let the other site know that you are there. It can be embarrassing to see and overhear something that was not intended for everyone. As with any meeting, introductions should be made while making sure each participant is visible when making his or her introduction. Also, establish ground rules – like avoid sidebar conversations, crinkling paper next to the microphone, turn off cell phones, etc.

- **Establish a facilitator.** This person will run the meeting and make sure the agenda is followed. He or she will also make opening and closing remarks.

- **Watch the remote locations.** When the room is equipped with monitors for both the remote and local sites, don't watch yourself on the monitor during the conference. Remember that the other side is watching you: You don't want to be viewed checking your hair or makeup, or doing anything unsightly. Focus your attention on the person speaking.

- **Pay attention to grooming.** The video camera magnifies you, especially high-definition feeds. What you wear and how you are groomed will be noticed. Visualize yourself projected on a big screen television: anything out of place is going to show up. It is best to avoid checks, plaids and overly bright colors.

- **Show consideration for others.** Speak in a normal

tone of voice; it's not necessary to shout to be heard. Most videoconferencing systems produce a slight delay of audio between sites. As a result, it is important to wait until the person speaking is finished before commenting. Talking over someone else will cause confusion – and it's rude.

Videoconference practice:

- **Prepare a five-minute presentation (subject doesn't matter) and videotape yourself.** Watch the tape several times and give yourself an honest critique. Then, tape yourself again and do the same thing. If you keep repeating the same mistakes, concentrate on improving them when you videotape yourself again. If you find yourself using power robbers while speaking (umm's, ah's, like, you know), keep practicing until you can speak smoothly for five minutes without using any. Then videotape yourself again. You may have to do this five or six times before you feel comfortable in front of the camera. If you are unhappy with how you look or your facial expressions, practice speaking in front of a mirror until you have eliminated the unwanted expressions. Then, videotape yourself again.

- **If you find yourself terrified of the camera, remember, being comfortable is not something that comes naturally to many people.** Even seasoned broadcasters admit to recurring stage fright. A series of relaxation exercises like the ones in chapter seven may help you to feel more in control.

- **Most people are uncomfortable looking at them-selves on camera.** The goal is to look comfortable and not detract from the visual message. Do this by having a natural hairstyle and makeup. Although the lights may make you look washed out, you don't want to look like you're going on the stage. A little more blush for women is usually all that's necessary. For men who perspire and shine when nervous, a light dusting of corn starch with a large brush on the nose, forehead, and chin can eliminate that shiny look.

- **What you wear also can distract from what you have to say.** For those on the other end of your videoconference, who may never have seen you before, this is going to be their only impression of you. Choose subdued or neutral colors appropriate to your style and coloring. Men and women should avoid bright, flashy colors and loud ties. Simple jewelry is appropriate; avoid dangling or jangling earrings, bracelets, or necklaces. For men, avoid ties with narrow, repeating stripes which can be distracting on camera. Depending on how the room is lit, glasses may cause a glare. If you wear glasses, select those with non-glare lenses and rims.

Internet meetings/Web conferences/Webinars

What do you get when you combine a corporate-world love of PowerPoint presentations with ever-tighter budgets and schedules?

Answer: online presentations.

It is now easy and affordable to have people spread all over the country or globe, watching a real-time presentation on their computers, while listening to a speaker as part of a teleconference.

It doesn't matter what you call them – Webinar, Web conference or Internet meeting – the newest venue for presentations is cyberspace. Web conferencing, also known as eMeetings (or E-meetings), is another alternative to face-to-face events for a growing number of businesses.

A study by International Data Corporation of Framingham, Massachusetts, says that Web-based conferencing could replace one in 10 business trips (or six trips a year).

Another study done by WorldCom Conferencing, a provider of audio, video and Internet conferencing, indicated that professionals who meet and work together using the Internet say it improves their job satisfaction and reduces stress. More than one third of the wired-savvy professionals surveyed said they participated in Web conferencing. This growing trend appears to be continuing, since more than 70 percent of managers and executives surveyed said they'd likely use Web conferencing. If you're thinking of joining this movement, you need to know some basics.

How it works

Internet meetings provide firms with multiple locations across large geographic areas the ability to host virtual gatherings -- reducing travel costs and increasing productivity. This type of presentation format combines audio elements with a traditional conference call, and PowerPoint or other visual aid software.

A hosted service provider and software, like WILink, Inc., WebEx, Evoke, Astound, etc., can issue e-mail invitations to attendees, providing all the relevant details (time, audio dial-in link information, and Web address/URL).

Just like with in-person presentations, the presenter can control what the audience members are seeing ... and has the ability to point and underline, and even write on the slides.

Participants "arrive" by clicking on the Web link provided. Conference organizers make audio available either through traditional phone lines (party calls), or streaming audio.

Audience members can view a presenter's slide show simultaneously, or any other files or demonstrations. Some Internet meeting software allows users to automatically make changes to documents online. Various providers also allow attendees to post questions live as text-based queries or on an "electronic whiteboard." Instant surveys of audience members can also be conducted, with results showing within minutes.

Many Web meeting providers also offer live chat features, and archiving of presentations to be viewed at a later date. Some Web conferencing hosts also allow users to participate in private discussions, breaking off from the main group.

Problem areas

Technology-related drawbacks to Web conferencing exist, including slow Internet connections, a busy Web, and a lack of broadcast-quality images.

Some issues arise due to the lack of speaker visuals – not seeing a presenter creates many challenges. Speakers need to put extra energy into their voices. Because audience members can't see you, they are going to rely more heavily on your voice for nonverbal clues. If you say you are excited about a project, they will need to hear that excitement in your voice. If you are like most people, your voice tends to lose some energy and get flat on the phone. Don't let this happen during an online presentation.

Reach out to your audience members more deliberately. Because they are invisible, you don't have visual signals like a questioning look or distracted behavior (i.e. pencil tapping). Even though the Webcast system allows for audience members to click on their screens and indicate they have questions, you need to take the initiative and ask for audience participation regularly.

Some experts fear that Internet meetings have a negative impact on the energy levels of participants, and eliminate the camaraderie and excitement an in-person sales meeting can achieve -- especially when there are team-building activities and motivational speakers.

It's important to realize that virtual meetings don't totally eliminate the need for one-on-one follow up at a later date, face-to-face. Some training needs to be done hands-on, for example ... the Web conference can share information, but "real world" training or coaching sessions need to be conducted in person.

Improve *Your* Next Online Event

If you're planning your first Web conference and don't know where to start, or are a veteran looking for ways to improve your online events, here are 12 ideas for delivering an online event, courtesy of WILink, Inc., a Richmond, Virginia-based company that enables customers to deliver online presentations, seminars and training either live (synchronous) or on-demand (asynchronous), using their Vcall Web Conferencing "web event solution" (www.vcall.com).

• **Get off to a fast start.** Don't you hate it when you attend a presentation and the emcee takes forever to introduce the main speaker? That effect is amplified many times over in a live Web event. Spend no more than two minutes to introduce your event, and cover the features of your host Web conferencing software. Then move aside and let the main presenter start. This will give your event a fast-paced feel that will keep participants tuned in.

• **Keep it short.** Live events of 60 to 90 minutes are most effective. If your program requires more time, consider breaking it into segments delivered over a period of days or weeks. Identify only the three or four key messages you want to leave with your audience, and build your presentation around them exclusively. In a 90-minute program, this will give you enough time to interact with the audience members, asking them questions and answering any they have.

• **Keep it simple.** It's easy to become enamored with all the features that Web conferencing systems offer. Avoid the temptation to try all the bells and whistles if you're just starting out, or if you're trying a new system. Master the basic controls: slide control, polling and messaging. Once you and your audience are comfortable with these elements, you can gradually introduce more sophisticated features that require more setup such as streaming audio, whiteboarding, and application broadcasting.

• **Ask good questions.** As you design your event, think about what you most want to get from the event. Use those goals to formulate the questions you want to ask of the audience. Don't use a live event to ask pointless demographic questions such as, "Where are you attending from?" That kind of information can be determined in pre-event registration. Use your time in front of your audience to ask questions that collect critical feedback and measure the effectiveness of your message.

• **Use a specialist.** For live events with more than 20 participants, use an "online specialist" to answer questions submitted by the audience while the speaker is presenting. The barriers to participation are low in an online event, so you can expect to receive more questions and comments than in a typical face-to-face presentation. Using a specialist means that everyone who asks a question will get a personalized response. This also allows your presenter to stay focused on delivering his or her key points without being distracted by a high volume of questions.

• **Pre-flight everyone.** Encourage all participants to complete a pre-flight check before attending your event. Pre-flight checks are usually Web pages provided by the event service provider that check the participant's computer to ensure it is capable of successfully participating in the program.

• **Start with the phone.** To ease people into the technology, use Web conferencing in conjunction with a familiar medium first, such as teleconferencing. Let the teleconference deliver the audio, and let the Web conference offer participants a way to see visual material and ask questions without interruptions. Use the interactive features of the teleconference bridge such as live question-and-answer sessions to simulate a radio "talk show" format. As your audience becomes comfortable with the basic elements of a Web conference, you can migrate some participants to Internet-based audio to reduce teleconference expense.

• **Keep slides simple.** Web conferencing works best when slides are formatted with simple designs and a few consistent colors. Don't use full-screen photos in your slides -- these images will take too long to display for participants. Flat colors and simple graphics, when made "Web ready" for your event, will display quickly on the screen.

• **Need to demonstrate a computer application to your audience?** Select a Web conferencing system that supports application broadcasting, and you can show the application directly from your computer. Practice with this many times before your event to get comfortable with how it works, and how it looks from your perspective and the audience's. You'll find that most systems require you to download and install a plug-in to capture and display what's on your screen.

• **Rent an emcee.** For important events, hire a professional online moderator who is familiar with the Web conferencing environment to facilitate your event. A moderator can add a great deal of polish to the many transitory tasks that occur during an event. For example, the moderator can coordinate interactive polls and talk with a presenter while waiting for results to come from the audience. This eliminates the awkward "dead air" that occurs when waiting for an audience to respond. A moderator can also make the question-and-answer process happen smoothly by asking prepared questions and gleaning the best questions from the audience for the speaker. Perhaps most importantly, these professionals know how to keep an online event moving when glitches occur, allowing speakers to focus on their message, rather than worry about which button to click.

• **Test, test and retest.** Once your event is staged and ready to go, make sure you test the "links" that will be sent to your registered participants. If the correct link isn't sent, your audience won't be able to find your event! Double-check the phone number for your teleconference for participants and presenters. Failure to check links and phone numbers are the most common mistakes made in producing Web events, and are completely preventable. On the day of the program, set up two computers. Set up one computer with your presenter's view and another logged on as an audience member. This gives you a much better sense of what your participants are experiencing. Slides that are slow may display quickly for the audience. This will also allow you to check the formatting and appearances of your visuals from the participant's perspective.

• **Finally, don't go looking for trouble.** Glitches can happen during any type of presentation, whether in person or over the Web. In Web-based events, glitches are often an issue if they are acknowledged by the presenter. For example, if you click a button to advance to the next slide and it is slow to change, you gain nothing by telling the audience, "Gosh this sure is taking a long time to come up." Perhaps you're on a slower-than-average Internet connection and the audience is receiving the slide before you do. Just make a mental note to advance slides a little sooner. When something doesn't work as expected, it is best to simply go on with the presentation and usually no one will be the wiser.

With these tips, your online presentations can be more than just efficient – they can be effective.

Part Eleven
Special Occasion Presentations

"I do not try to be better than anybody else. I only try to be better than myself."
-- **Dan Jansen,** Olympic gold medalist

In the course of your career, you will probably find yourself called upon to speak at a special occasion. Unlike an informative or persuasive presentation, often the goal of a speaking at a special occasion is to be inspirational or motivational, so choosing the right words and coming across to your audience as sincere are essential. Using colorful language will help you to express your thoughts about the occasion. Your words should arouse emotion and focus the audience's thoughts and feelings on whom or what is being honored or commemorated. If you read your speech from note cards, you will not seem sincere, therefore, it is essential that you know your key points and introduction cold.

When speaking at a special occasion, your technique and organizational skills are less important than at other kinds of presentations because there are clear expectations of what your speech should contain. For example: If you are honoring a recently promoted executive, the audience will expect to hear about his or her accomplishments and awards, possibly a humorous anecdote about the person, and perhaps that person's new or future responsibilities within the company. If you were presenting at a roast, you would expect to be telling stories at the honoree's expense. All in fun and good taste, of course.

Some speakers prefer to start their speeches with a joke. Jokes can grab an audience's attention, but unless you are extremely comfortable using humor and are positive that your humor will be appreciated -- and that it is really funny -- you should not tell jokes when asked to speak at a special occasion. That does not mean you won't be able to use humor; it simply means that jokes are best left to professionals.

When you are asked to speak at a special occasion, it may be to introduce other speakers, speak at testimonials, banquets or ceremonials, or deliver welcome or exit speeches, perhaps even a eulogy. It is important for you to understand what is expected of you, and for you to perform accordingly.

Welcome presentation

The welcome presentation is designed to welcome people into companies or organizations, or groups to conferences, and is generally a short speech used to begin an event or occasion. This type of presentation sets the mood and flow of upcoming events, and outlines the occasion for the audience members so they know what to expect. The expectation is to associate the values of the welcoming group or individual with those values possessed by the person or people being welcomed.

Example: "Good morning associates, family, and friends. The Board of Directors and I would like to welcome you to our first annual employee and family day. Today will give all of you, and all of us, the opportunity to learn about each other and our families as we join in games and activities designed to further the goals of our company."

Welcome speeches are also used for wedding receptions, awards banquets, and dinner receptions, and they tend to have a strong impact on the audience. It gives the event organizers, hosts, or sponsors an opportunity to show who they are and what the event is about, and sets the tone. The welcome speech is an opportunity for you to distinguish yourself. If you do a good job welcoming your boss to his or her anniversary dinner, you may find yourself asked to give more presentations.

Speeches of introduction

A strong introduction should generate enthusiasm and

give audience members a quick overview of the person they are about to encounter. It should include accurate information and enhance the impression of the person about to make his or her way to the platform. A good introduction generates excitement and enthusiasm for the upcoming speaker or performer, and makes the audience receptive to what is going to be said or done.

Example: "Marjorie Brody has a secret. This secret has led her from the quiet life of a college professor to the platform of some of the world's most prestigious organizations. Marjorie Brody knows the secret of using personal marketing to make life-changing events happen. Today, she is going to share that secret with you, and then you will be able to change your life as well."

An introduction that detracts something from the person being presented or his or her presentation can ruin the entire event. Be careful not to give misleading, useless, speculative or untrue information. Finally, be sure you pronounce the person's name correctly. When in doubt, ask for the correct pronunciation before you go out in front of the audience, and write it out phonetically. If you are being introduced it is a good idea to write your own introduction and send it in advance to the person doing the introduction. Bring an extra copy to the event.

Acceptance speeches

You've just won "Employee of the Year" at your company, and during the luncheon in your honor, you will be making an acceptance speech. This isn't the Academy Awards®, and it's also not the time to be dramatic. Be sincere and let your thanks be heartfelt. Thank the person or people giving you the award, and anyone who inspired or helped you, including your family. A gracious and sincere acceptance speech will be remembered, and you will be seen in a positive light. Acceptance speeches are common in the world of business, politics and entertainment.

Example: "I feel like I have grown up at BRODY Professional Development. And it's been a wonderful experience for me. Today, you are honoring me by naming me Employee of the Year -- but I would also like to honor you. Having the opportunity to be a part of a company like BRODY Professional Development has taught me about the important things in a career – the opportunity to grow, to experience loyalty, to develop my skills, and to be appreciated for them. To my co-workers and to those who granted me this honor today, I say, "Thank you."

Inauguration speech

Usually given by a person who is assuming the head of an organization or government. They can include those delivered by the incoming president of a club or the president of an association. The objectives in this type of presentation are to reaffirm the values of the organization you are about to head, and to state the goals you will attempt to achieve while in that position.

Some goals to keep in mind: Note the accomplishments of your predecessor; highlight your own accomplishments without bragging; include the direction you and your team would like to take; make everyone there want to be on your team.

Eulogies

If you are asked to say a few words at a eulogy about someone you have worked with (or for), keep your remarks short and tactful. Although you and Jim might have had some great times after work at the corner pub, this is not the time to mention them. Be respectful of the family, and remember that your boss may be there listening (and judging you).

Example: "Jim and I spent the past 15 years working side by side at Plaza Computers. He was a thoughtful co-worker and good friend. I will miss sharing ideas with him and learning from Jim ... ."

The toastmaster or master of ceremonies

This is the person who conducts the event. This type of an occasion can be a company dinner, retirement party, roast, birthday, or even an event for visiting delegations of some kind (students, politicians, foreign visitors, etc.). It is the responsibility of the toastmaster to play a leading part in running the show. He or she makes sure everything goes smoothly and stays on time, and also plays a part as master of ceremonies or moderator. The toastmaster gives the opening remarks, leads the group into the meal (if applicable), introduces other speakers and closes the event. If awards are to be handed out, the toastmaster may perform that role as well or introduce those who will be doing it. If there is to be a question-and-answer period, it is also the job of the toastmaster to facilitate this as well. The toastmaster should communicate in advance with other speakers to make certain procedures are clear and to assign time slots. If things drag, the toastmaster should tactfully step in or alert the speaker that time is running out. It is also up to the toastmaster to avoid putting anyone on the spot who does not wish to speak. This is especially true during ceremonies where those honored are surprised and may not wish to speak.

New employee orientations

These events are often coordinated by the human resources department in large companies. As part of an orientation program, you may be asked to speak to a group of new employees or trainees. Get specific information as to what is expected of you, who else will be speaking, and the topics they will be covering, and the amount of time you have for your presentation. You will be giving the new employees information about your area of expertise, and your presentation should take into account the limited amount of knowledge they may have about how things work at the company. This is an occasion to provide information, and to generate a positive impression of yourself and your department. As you will probably be presenting as part of a group, respect the time constraints. If there will not be enough time to answer questions, offer new employees a best method or time to contact you for additional information. If you will be representing your department, check with others you work with to see if they would like you to include any information you may not have thought of.

The farewell speech

These speeches are commonplace today, as people change jobs and careers frequently. If you will be speaking on your own departure, mention some of the memorable experiences you shared with the people there and indicate how these experiences have contributed to your growth and enjoyment. It's a time you can single out people who made a significant contribution to your work experience and thank them. If you are speaking about someone else who is leaving, pay tribute to him or her by recognizing that person's contributions to the company.

Using stories & anecdotes

When a businessperson is asked to speak at a special occasion, you are not expected to be the entertainment.

But you can use humor naturally by telling your own stories and anecdotes. It is a good idea for you to compile your own humorous stories, or others you have heard that you will feel comfortable sharing. An advantage of telling your own stories is that they help to build audience rapport. This is true with co-workers and employees who will see you in a new light as you share a part of yourself. If the stories are work-related and you all work in the same firm or industry, there will be a unique feeling of relating – you to the audience members and they to you as you share your story. Your stories need not be strictly work-related, however.

You can use humorous anecdotes from your own life, for example:
- trips you have taken
- your family
- your childhood
- your own career path
- your hobbies
- your friends
- your own embarrassing moments
- your fears

By sharing your own personal stories, you will quickly make a connection with listeners, and they will be more receptive to whatever comes next in your presentation. A word of caution: If you are delivering a special occasion speech that is negative, like company downsizing or a reduction in stock price, this is not the time to begin with a humorous anecdote.

Part Twelve

Meet the Pros

*"I want to be remembered as a person who felt there was no limi-
tation to what the human body and mind can do, and be the
inspiration to lead people to do things they never hoped to do."*
-- **Carl Lewis,** Olympic track and field star, winner of nine
gold medals, one silver medal

One of the most beneficial things I do for myself as a
professional speaker is observe other professional
speakers at work and solicit their opinions about relevant subjects. To give you the benefit of other speakers'
knowledge and experience, I have asked some of the
top speaking and training professionals around to share
their own methods and tips for success in a variety of
situations. Their contact information is included, if
you would like to reach them.

Effectively Conducting Software and Online Demonstrations
By Michele Remey Pepe

Many companies offer software and Internet solutions
for their external clients and internal colleagues.
Usually, getting people to buy into using these solutions involves showing how they work and explaining
the benefits of the technology. Software and online

demonstrations are a frequent part of many sales and trade-show presentations. Yet, these types of presentations are fraught with challenges. For example, should an online solution be shown "live" or should it be a simulation? If multiple computers, servers, and networks would be involved in this series of tasks in an actual office environment, how can it effectively be demonstrated using only one or two PCs?

Unfortunately, technology provides the perfect opportunity for proving Murphy's Law. If you think two systems will "talk" to each other for your demo, think again. If you want to show your client the ease and speed of your solution, today will be the day when everything moves slower than molasses. If you think your solution is very "user-friendly," today is the day when the village idiot will show up and be the guinea pig for the group. If you think you know the system inside out, today it will find a new way to challenge you -- something you've not dealt with before.

So what can you do to be over-prepared and thwart Murphy's Technology Law at every turn? The following are some tips to help you effectively prepare for, and ultimately conduct, software and online demos.

Tips to effectively conduct software and online demonstrations:

• **Set up everything before the demonstration day.** Run through certain parts of the demo ahead of time, and see how things are working. Clear up any problems that arise.

• **Know what the possible glitches in the demo model could be. What will you say when one arises?** It is best to explain what is happening and why. Usually it's because the demo computer is showing multi-user/multi-computer functions at once, and this slows down the processing or transfer of data. If you don't address the situation, the audience will still see it and wonder if it's a usual problem with the software, and not just something unique to the demo. Also, depending on the kind of Internet connection available to you for an online demonstration, you may experience delays in the transfer of data. It is best to be honest about what is happening, and explain that certain circumstances are out of your product's control. Don't make excuses for your demo model, just explain that sometimes this happens and tell the observers what is going on.

• **Is it live? Or is it a simulation? How does this effect what the client would see in real life? How is it the same, and how is it different?** Address these questions up front. If you are simulating Internet-related software, why? Many people will assume it's because your online product doesn't really work -- you may have to explain that it's because of pre-prepared data you need to take advantage of, or some other real-world challenge that is not within your control. By doing a simulation, you are maintaining control in order to give the group the best example of how the product really works.

• **Have a "two-headed" demo whenever possible: e.g., one person to "drive" the software, and one person to facilitate the group.** It can be very challenging to drive the software, present the information, and facilitate a group. By having two people involved, the responsibilities can be shared and more effectively managed. This is also helpful for when glitches arise -- one person can fix the glitch and the other can bring up something else of interest to the group (to divert attention).

• **Think ahead about who is in the room.** Consider what they want from your presentation. If there are executives and decision makers present, remember, they want the facts and the bottom line. Your fellow technology folks will want all of the gory details. Your end-users may be clueless about why they're there and what they're seeing. They just want to know how the product will help them in their roles, and that they'll be able to learn these new skills. Finally, remember, there may be consultants and other outside-the-company professionals in the room helping your clients make their decision. What's on their minds? More business. You must include them in some of your comments, and at the very least, not discount the strength of their input to decision makers.

• **Have a general outline of the demonstration topics that you and the other person will review.** Determine ahead of time who will cover which portions of the presentation. Also discuss if it is OK to "jump in" during the other person's presentation. Some presenters will welcome this kind of open exchange, while others will find it disruptive. Agree, however, that if a problem arises with the software -- such as a long start-up process or a glitch -- one person will pick up the presentation topic and run with it while the other navigates the software crisis.

• **Start with some background and context for the viewers.** Build a story around what they are seeing. What is the situation, who is the user, and what are they doing? You may want to use PowerPoint to support the context, especially if you are highlighting only a small part of a larger process, such as the employee who uses a travel expense report, or the user who creates product change orders. PowerPoint slides can also be used to highlight the benefit statements at the beginning and summarize them again at the end.

• **Some clients will say that they do not want to see PowerPoint slides because they think you are hiding behind a visual aid rather than showing your product.** If your client has specified "no PowerPoint" consider other ways to create the context or keep the PowerPoint slides to a minimum of two or three. Let the demo be the focus.

• **If you are presenting alone, get up and stop running the demo every now and then.** People will become bored and distracted if you are continually seated behind a monitor. Sitting down for long periods of time will also reduce your control of the group and authority. Standing up every 10 to 15 minutes or so will accomplish two things: one, it will wake up the group and draw its attention back to you, and two, it will allow you to regain focus and interact with the group.

• **If the aspect of the demo you are showing takes a minute to launch, type first to get it started, and then stop to talk with the group while the startup is happening.** Remember to type first, then talk. Have questions prepared for the group.

• **Close "windows" along the way.** Don't leave multiple screens open as they will create a distraction. Also, hit any prompts, such as "OK" that may come up. Don't leave them sitting on the screen. These will be a distraction to your viewers.

• **Use client-specific examples and speak in terms of "you" or "this person," rather than "I."** During demonstrations, some presenters say, "What I am doing now," or "What I want to do next is …" It is more effective to say, "What the IT administrator would do now is …" or "What you would be looking for is … ." Remember, you are playing roles to demonstrate how clients would use the software. If you continue to say "I," they will have a harder time making the connection to their world.

• **Speak in terms of benefits.** Sometimes the presenters will get caught up in the features of the product -- "what it does." However, what will sell the product are its benefits -- "why it's important." The product's benefits are the answer to the question: "So what?" Think and speak in terms of four kinds of benefits: Quality, Quantity, Money and Time. These are four consistent areas of benefits that everyone finds interesting. How will this better the quality of work, or our end product? Does this create more output, or less downtime? Will we save money or make money? Will this save time or more efficiently use time? Remember, users and administrators are looking for benefits at a personal or project level, whereas executives tend to look at benefits more from a broader organizational level. Speak in these terms. When you find yourself citing features, ask yourself, "So what?"

• **Create benefit statements that address multiple levels of the audience at the same time: executives, end users, IT administrators, finance, operations, etc.** For example, "This reporting tool enables the user to coordinate related data in an efficient and streamlined fashion, saving hours of time. Imagine the effect this efficiency will have across the organization as we save time for all of your operations people, and, therefore, allow their efforts to be focused on other critical company initiatives rather than data entry." This sentence illustrates the proper way to state benefits at a user and executive level.

• **Remember that specifics and details show a certain knowledge level more than general and vague statements.** Do not get so bogged down in the details, however, that you lose some people in the room. Save some of these details for any questions that may arise. If a technology person wants to know the specifics of the system, respond briefly and specifically. This will do two things: one, it will answer his or her question, and two, it will set you up as a credible expert because you could answer the question specifically. If the details will take a long time to explain, just give a short version and then offer to speak with the person in more detail during a break. Remember that your "non-tech" audience members (some executives and end-users) will not be able to keep up with that discussion, and you don't want to leave anyone behind.

• **Get group members involved -- ask questions and get them to tell you about their reality.** When you come to a screen with choices, ask them: "What would you want to do next?" or "What is the first thing you look for?" or "What icons on here do you already recognize?" If possible, try to allow someone from the group to use part of the demo.

• **Tell stories and use examples along the way.** These will strongly illustrate how your product actually functions in the real world. I know of one professional who told a story about trying to change a confidential password for an important employee who had just resigned. It happened on a Friday, when this IT person was out of town. He couldn't change the password for this person from a remote location, so he had to go into work over the weekend. During his product demo, he explained how the people could access and manipulate the data from a remote location using this software -- with ease and without delay. His story helped bring the situation alive for many audience members. Remember to continually create the context of what they are seeing, and how it would affect their reality.

• **Do not be afraid of repetition.** Audience members are not paying attention 100% of the time. You can remind them of things as you go, such as, "As I mentioned before, this is a simulation of the software, so it would be faster when you use it." Repetition is a helpful memory technique.

• **Remember, the group will reflect the presenter's demeanor.** If you are excited about your product, let it show through your words and animation. You don't have to bounce around the room, but do allow your enthusiasm for the technology to show. Speak in positive terms, do not bash the competition, and do not rush through parts of the demo that you think are dull. If you are bored by the demo or think it's a "dry topic," your audience will absorb and reflect your lack of enthusiasm as well.

Software and online demonstrations should be exciting events for the presenter and viewer. They are positive opportunities for you and your company to showcase the solutions you have for clients. Remember, people are your listeners and viewers. Too many presenters who deal with technology expect their audience to be as linear, well-defined, and rational as the solutions they are presenting. People have logical and emotional reasons for working with your company, and its proposed product solution. Decision makers have business needs and personal needs for making the best decision for the given situation. Sometimes we think, "If it is the best solution, they should buy it." Of course, this is not always the case.

If you interact with your audience as real people with real issues that are not always rational, and if you understand and address these issues, you will be farther along your way to success.

Michele Remey Pepe is a senior consultant with BRODY Professional Development. She specializes in the areas of leadership, management development, and team performance. She can be reached at 800-726-7936.

Ten Tips for Presenting Technical Material to Management Audiences
by William R. Steele

When conducting a course on presentation skills, it's common to have participants ask about the challenge of presenting technical material to nontechnical audiences. Their biggest concern is with presentations given to "management."

To hear the management people talk, this concern is well-founded. Technical presentations often frustrate them. Time and again, they find themselves on the receiving end of a "data dump," buried in technical jargon instead of enlightened.

When a technical presenter faces a management audience, it's like the meeting of two different worlds. Language, context, knowledge base, and priorities can all be different. The successful technical presenter steps over into the audience's world, and gives an audience-centered presentation. The presenter becomes an interpreter who translates the technical message for the audience members, making sure their needs drive the process.

Here are 10 tips that can help any technical presenter develop this ability:

1. Less is More. It's not how much information you give out that counts, but how much the audience comprehends and retains. The all-important question is, "What did they walk away with?"

Ironically, with nontechnical audiences, the transfer of knowledge is often in direct inverse proportion to the amount of technical detail given. Management finds it difficult to digest a detail-heavy presentation that, for an audience of fellow technical experts, might be just right.

Management wants the essential information needed to make an overall assessment and subsequent decisions. Have the back-up science, engineering and math available, but don't automatically include all these details in your presentation.

2. Don't Forget: It's a Jungle to Them. When presenting technical information, it's easy to forget that the management audience's familiarity with it is likely to be less than yours – less in-depth. You have been immersed in the subject; they have not. Preview. Provide multiple internal summaries. Review. You are a tour guide; don't charge through this "jungle" of information and lose the audience along the way.

3. Don't Assume They Understand. It is reasonable to assume that people who have made it into upper-level management are smart. What is not reasonable to assume is that these people will instantly understand all the technical concepts included in your presentation -- or that they will say something if they don't.

Assume that your audience will benefit from extra efforts to make things understandable. An extra example, analogy, or rephrased explanation, helps more often than it hurts. Your audience is more likely to become frustrated by a lack of understanding than impatient with your extra efforts.

4. Keep Referring to What They Already Know.
Understanding and memory are based on association. You can improve both for your audience members by relating new material back to what they already know. Highlight similarities; point out notable differences.

Note: When a management decision is needed, consider referring to similar or related decisions made in the past. Such references can not only help with understanding, they can increase comfort with the requested decision.

5. Use Visuals and Simplify. The old saying, "A picture is worth a thousand words" certainly holds true with technical presentations. With visuals, comprehension not only improves, it speeds up (no small consideration given the notorious impatience of management).

Keep in mind, however, the "picture" that's worth "a thousand words" is just that -- a picture. It's not paragraphs from a script, or your notes in bullet-point form, projected on the screen primarily to help you. A visual is most effective when it is a graphical (i.e. pictorial) representation.

Also, simplicity is essential. If management's quick comprehension is the objective, complexity is the enemy. If something is unavoidably complex, consider a building process over several visuals.

6. Hold "Lingo" to the Necessary Minimum. Spend enough time in a technical specialty, and you will end up speaking a language few people outside that specialty can understand. Loaded with lingo, buzz words, jargon, technical terms, and acronyms, this language will become second nature, so familiar its use is unconscious. Strive to speak in a language that everyone in your audience will understand. If possible, preview your presentation with someone outside your specialty who can point out language problems you may have missed.

When technical terms are unavoidable, and using acronyms makes sense for convenience, explain them when they first come up. If there are many of them, consider providing a reference key on a flip chart or in a handout.

7. Welcome Interaction and Adapt. Management audiences will often interrupt presentations with comments, questions, and discussions. For the presenter set on getting through complex technical material, this can be frustrating. The tendency is to doggedly plow on as opportunities to speak present themselves.

Instead of viewing audience involvement as something to struggle with, plan for it and make use of this participation. Prepare a flexible presentation that does not require all the allotted time. Then, since you are freed of time pressures, listen for the valuable feedback audience involvement provides. Do listeners understand the material? What needs to be re-explained? What can be skipped? What priorities are audience members revealing?

Getting through your prepared material, despite interruptions, does not define success -- effectively responding to the needs and desires of the audience does.

8. Demonstrate. When possible, take a step beyond verbal descriptions and pictures; actually demonstrate what you are talking about. The impact on the audience can be dramatic, increasing both comprehension and memorability.

Keep in mind, however, passing things around the room for close inspection is not a good idea during your presentation. Audience members will inevitably pay more attention to what is being passed around than to you. Although management types may ask to see items right away -- and their wishes cannot be ignored -- it's best to promise opportunities for later inspection.

9. Do the Unexpected. Management audiences will often walk into a technical presentation with a "here we go again" cynicism. The speaker faces distracted, inattentive, impatient people.

Part of the problem is the boiler-plate nature of so

many technical presentations. In the name of protocol they slavishly follow a long-established formula. No one can remember when this formula was originally adopted -- or why. What in all likelihood is an old-fashioned rut is either unconsciously followed or rationalized as the "proper/approved/standard" way these presentations have always been done.

You are only going to succeed if you capture your audience's attention. This is going to be hard if your presentation is indistinguishable from the hundreds that have preceded it.

While being sensitive to what is officially required, look for opportunities to do something new, different, unexpected. It doesn't have to be radical, just imaginative enough to pique some interest.

10. Sell! Ask a room full of technical presenters how many are in sales and few, if any, hands will go up. In truth, everybody is in sales.

Stressing benefits is the essence of sales. Convincing audience members they will benefit from what is being presented is the key to holding their attention.

Do not assume that the value of what you are saying is self-evident. Point out the value. Point out the benefits. Point out the possibilities. If your audience members don't desire the information you are providing (i.e. are not being "sold" on its value), they are not going to try to absorb it. If you want to be more successful making technical presentations to nontechnical, management audiences, keep these 10 tips in mind. They'll help you bridge the communication gap. And, remember, the key to all effective communication is being tuned into your audience.

William R. Steele is a senior training associate at BRODY Professional Development. He facilitates training programs and executive coaching sessions in presentation skills. He developed the "Speaking to Lead" course for BRODY. Bill can be contacted at 800-726-7936.

Presenting Around the World
By Michele Remey Pepe

Presentations in front of groups are challenging enough, let alone when there are multiple cultures and several languages in the room. What is critical to the success of an international presentation?

First, consider the basics. In all presentations, you must consider your communication signals -- the Visual, Vocal and Verbal impact. When presenting internationally, these cues are even more important.

Visually, you must present a polished image. Other

cultures, especially in Europe and Asia, will tend to be more formal than the United States in their dress and meeting interactions.

Come dressed in your business professional suit -- this shows respect for your audience. Wear darker, more conservative colors and cuts, depending on what is the most conservative look for your industry. When considering other visual areas of impact, remember that your visual aids, handouts, and all company materials must look very professional, neat and well organized. Again, this will strengthen the credibility of your organization and will demonstrate an attention to detail, both of which are critical statements about your company's abilities and intentions.

Whenever you are presenting, there will be multiple languages and dialects in the room. These present some **vocal** challenges. Everyone has an accent of some kind. Your best bet is to begin by apologizing for your "American accent." Realize that to others around the world, the American accent is not pretty, nor is it easy to listen to. We stress different syllables and we have regional influences that make things even more challenging to an international audience, most of whom are probably more used to hearing and speaking "British English," rather than "American English."

Speak at a moderate pace -- not so slowly that it is insulting to audience members, but not too quickly that they can't keep up. Pause frequently to give the audience a chance to translate what you've said and digest it. Vary your volume and inflection somewhat, but not too much -- Americans are often perceived as "emotional" and as "exaggerated" because of our animated voices. Finally, when asking the group for questions or input, expect to pause a little longer than you might for American audience members. Remember, they have to translate what you said, digest it, determine what their questions may be, and finally translate it into English. That can take time, so be patient and prepared to wait for questions and comments.

Your last communication signal is the **verbal** -- your content. Avoid using idioms or colloquialisms in your speech. Phrases such as "pass the buck," "right off the bat," or "wait till the cows come home" would work with many American audiences, but can confuse international audiences.

Your international audience members who speak English as their second language -- or sometimes third or fourth language ("international English") -- will be translating literally, so phrases like these won't make sense. In a presentation to an audience composed of different nationalities, one trainer I know was discussing the "stage hog" as a member of an audience, and someone in the room from Asia raised his hand and asked, "I'm sorry, did you say that there are pigs sitting in the meeting?" The term "hog" as a reference for a person didn't make sense, and the speaker had to clarify what he meant. Use the precise word for what you mean, and avoid slang and casual expressions that are sprinkled throughout American speech.

Your sentences should be relatively short. Avoid connecting everything you say with "and" or "but." International audiences will be working to organize your message in chunks, and if you speak in run-on sentences, your audience will become confused. Have all of your content in professional handouts -- many people can read English more easily than they can speak it or listen to it.

Finally, use visual aids to reinforce the main points of what you are saying. PowerPoint slides with graphics and text can be very helpful. Keep the text short and to the point -- you don't want to lose your audience by having too much to read. Check ahead of time about what equipment will be available to you. Remember that if you choose to use videotape of any kind, the VHS system is prevalent in the United States, but the PAL system is more prevalent in Europe and parts of Asia. Plan a back-up way of using visuals, either transparencies or handouts, just in case your computer doesn't interact well with the local projection systems.

Using interpreters

If you must work through an interpreter, discuss the presentation ahead of time with him or her. Be sure that he or she understands the essence of what you are going to communicate -- sometimes a literal translation is not effective. Address the group directly when you speak, and pause between chunks of information to give the interpreter time to communicate with the group. Find ways to have him or her ask questions of the group, or to have group members communicate back their understanding of what was said. By finding ways to "check-in" on the audience understanding, you can be sure that your message is being communicated properly through the interpreter.

Audience interaction and discussion

Interaction and discussion will be critical when presenting internationally. First, encourage the group to ask questions and participate in a discussion with you. This may take a few attempts on your part to truly gain interaction, because audiences outside of the United States tend to be more reserved and more formal during presentations -- they let the speaker speak. By building interaction into your presentation's introduction, and stopping periodically to check-in with the group, you will create a more interactive environment.

Another option is to have participants discuss a topic or issue with a person next to them, and then have them contribute their discussion to the meeting. This is a very helpful technique, especially when you have many different languages and cultures in one room. Some participants will feel self-conscious about their use of English, and may not want to participate. People will feel more comfortable if they have a partner to talk with first, and then to contribute to the group as a whole.

Taking questions

When taking questions and concluding discussions, repeat what was said and summarize key points. Try to say things the same way each time. In American presentations, we tend to substitute different words for the same thing. For example, a speaker might refer to an upcoming company meeting in a variety of ways such as a "conference," an "event," a "session," a "program," or a "get-together." In American presentations, this is fine because the audience understands that the speaker is referring to the same meeting each time. However, international audiences may not realize this and may think that each word represents a different meeting. Using the same words and phrases in the same way each time lets the repetition confirm what was heard, allowing audience members to understand it correctly.

Details to remember

Finally, consider certain housekeeping items when presenting internationally. Consider ahead of time where to seat people as they arrive. More senior participants should be seated toward the front of the room. Group together more senior people and language similarities -- this will help create a more comfortable atmosphere. Plan to conduct introductions as participants arrive -- either you or a colleague of yours should greet participants, conduct introductions and guide people to their seats. Always distribute an agenda at the start of the presentation. This printed piece will tell the group when any breaks will be and explain the day's events. Plan breaks no more than 90-minutes apart -- for participants who are smokers and may want more frequent and slightly longer breaks. Ask that all cell phones be turned off or muted for the presentation. Say that if someone needs to make or receive a call that he or she may step outside of the room to do so.

The following list reviews some of the key points about presenting around the world:

Speak distinctly and at a measured pace. Avoid humor or sarcasm, as it may not translate well.

Use simple, clear handouts for your audience to follow along. It is easier for people who know "international English" to read them.

Use notes -- it means you are prepared and not "winging it."

Repeat key points and summarize periodically.

Invite questions. Tell group members it will help both you and them "succeed" today if they ask questions.

Ask that they forgive your accent. Ask if you are speaking loud enough so that everyone can hear.

Pay attention to your appearance and the appearance of all materials and handouts. Everything should be of good quality.

Other pointers for communicating internationally

When listening to international English ...

• **Repeat what you believe was said and ask for verification** that you heard correctly.

• **Ask questions to clarify.** Also, many cultures expect verbal and nonverbal "prompts" to show that you are listening. After you've answered a question, ask, "What other questions do you have about that?"

• **Summarize key points and action items.**

• **Mirror audience members' level of eye contact and other body language.**

• **Take notes if you say you will get back to someone.** Do not write on business cards, however.

Michele Remey Pepe is a senior consultant with BRODY Professional Development. She specializes in the areas of leadership, management development, and team performance. She can be reached at 800-726-7936.

When Speechwriters Make the Difference
By Bob Stewart

Our attempts to persuade someone to hire us to write speeches for them or others sometimes resemble selling personal insurance. "I don't think so," says the client. "Look, everybody knows how to write. Thanks, but I'll take my chances."

Opinions about well-written speeches, and who's qualified to write them, are like cell phones; everybody's got one ... and sometimes nobody answers when "wanna be" speechwriters practice personal versions of "Can you hear me now?"

There are plenty of convincing reasons why others should hire us to research and write speeches instead of recalling their mothers' singing, "Anything you can do, I can do better" from Broadway's classic, "Annie Get Your Gun!"

So, what should we tell them? "I'm sure you write well and are confident you can write your own speeches. You also ought to consider some practical reasons for letting qualified professionals write speeches for executives in your organization. Good speechwriters ... I"m talking about really good ones ... know how to":

Keep a speech's message on course instead of rambling aimlessly. Sometimes you're too close to your own message – words wander, losing their direction and the audience's attention quickly. Good speechwriters make sure your message's style, pace, and tone are clear and concise from beginning to end. All parts of the speech are understandable and logically connected. The speechwriter also can be objective when you necessarily can't, and still remain faithful to the emotional spirit and theme for your primary message.

Poised and confident speakers count for a lot. But they won't find any cover from a badly composed, poorly written speech and an unforgiving audience.

Write for the listener rather than the reader. The executive producer of "ABC World News Tonight" might enjoy reading newspaper columns written by acclaimed national journalists. But he or she wouldn't ask Thomas Friedman or Ellen Goodman or George Will to write the copy that scrolls on Charlie Gibson's teleprompter five nights a week. There is a distinct difference between both styles and voices of writing. Friedman, Will, and Goodman would tell Gibson's producer that while appreciating the offer, they didn't perfect their craft in that venue.

Keep the speech aimed at the audience's expectations. What audience members come and want to hear always counts more than what a speaker wants to hear himself or herself say. It's about them, not the speaker. Professional speechwriters know how to craft a narrative message so its impact does not stray from what the audience expects, and the speaker wants to express.

Respect the rules of grammar and elements of style. Speeches and official remarks at least ought to pass English Composition 101, not some tortured representation of America's primary language. Speechwriters know, and remember, that adverbs modify verbs and adjectives, along with the rules of parallel construction and consistent verb tense. A speech that's supposed to inspire, while it mangles the rules of grammar and narrative construction, ends up a pathetic collection of brutally disjointed words and phrases.

Effectively compose the dominant thoughts in the speaker's head and heart. The speech's rhythm should be coherent, the overall message eloquent, memorable, and its vocabulary rich rather than annoyingly repetitious. A veteran speechwriter can craft words and phrases that will reflect a speaker's beliefs as even-handed instead of small-minded; lasting, not some editorial disappearing act.

I was once asked to consider writing speeches for the chairman of a major pharmaceutical and health care company. The question was natural; I'd already written speeches for a prominent U.S. governor and high visibility communications for the drug and health care industry. The other person said, "I ought to tell you we consider this to be a junior position. It probably won't even be at the managerial level in the organization."

A week later a friend asked me what I thought about the encounter. I answered that if they offered the job, I'd thank them but pass on it. It seemed to me they didn't think the person who wrote the words of a leading American business executive was worth much, literally and philosophically. Most of all, I believed it represented how little they valued their chairman's message.

I'd listened several times to the same chairman and the company's president/CEO address their employees worldwide on satellite or closed circuit television. Their words were wooden and superficial, seeming void of genuine feeling and commitment. Each time I was particularly unmoved by what they said, how they said it, and felt sorry for the speechwriter who owned the script.

On one episode of NBC's former political drama, "The West Wing," the character of speechwriter played actor Rob Lowe claimed, "Oratory should raise your heart rate. Oratory should blow the doors off the place." I think so too, and expect my speechwriting colleagues would agree.

We should tell our prospective client that if he or she needed heart surgery, they'd ask a cardiovascular surgeon, not their family doctor, to perform the procedure. When someone is scheduled to deliver a speech or remarks, serious or lighthearted, official or conversational to any waiting audience, he or she should call on a professional speechwriter to write it ... not on personal pride and vanity to wing it.

Bob Stewart has written speeches for the Governor of New Jersey, the presidents and CEOs of national trade associations, business leaders, and political candidates. He also crafted speeches and other key editorial messages for a major health care initiative involving legal reforms and federal legislation, to improve patient safety and compensation associated with prescription medicines and biologics. He can be reached at 732-238-9279, and at good4prose@gmail.com.

Speaking to Lead & Inspire
By William R. Steele

A commonly held belief is that speaking as a leader is something that only a few people can do. In reality, it is a learnable skill that revolves around a consistent, well-defined speech structure.

"Change" is the Guiding Concept

The call for leadership comes with a need for change. This focus on change, in turn, determines the approach a leader takes in developing a message.

In its simplest form, the approach to leadership speaking involves two steps:

1) defining reality

2) establishing the vision

First Comes the Agreement on Reality

Leadership expert Warren Bennis says, "The first task of a leader is to define reality." It's the first task because no group of people, no audience, will accept a leader's prescription for change unless it first accepts the leader's description of the reality that is being faced. In other words, people must agree with the "what is" message before they'll accept "what must be."

This concept is illustrated when political leaders engage in debate. If the subject is campaign finance reform, for example, one side will paint a picture of a political system corrupted by money. The opposing side will speak of free speech and an active citizenry. Those who believe the first group's definition of reality buy into new restrictions on political spending. Those more swayed by the second side's description of "the way it is," are more inclined to buy into a vision of limited government interference.

The accepted way for a leader to establish reality is to begin by speaking about the past and then to move into a description of the present. Author Terry Pearce, who lectures on leadership and communication at the University of California, Berkeley, suggests thinking of this as a message that begins with "the way it was" and transitions into "the way it is." These two segments, together, constitute the speaker's reality message.

Then Comes the Vision

After establishing reality by speaking about the past and present, a leader then moves into describing what he or she thinks the future should be. This is commonly referred to as the speaker's vision. Pearce refers to it as "the way it will be."

Unlike what many people think, this vision does not have to be brilliant and innovative in order to be inspirational. The inspiration comes from the leader's communication of the vision in a way that captures both the hearts and minds of the listeners, and causes them to take ownership of it.

They Need to See the Big Picture and Hear it Personalized

A leader's message of change should both "paint the big picture" and explain how audience members fit into it. The result is a personalized big picture.

Most people go day to day focused primarily on their own immediate world; it's only natural. When forces affecting the organization create the need for change, they may not accept this need unless their leader gives them what some people call the "30,000 foot view." They need some help seeing what the leader sees, and understanding why change is necessary.

Then, to be fully effective, the big picture has to be

brought down to where they live (i.e., personalized). In other words, the leader can't stay at the 30,000 foot level; he or she also needs to explain what it all means to the individual listener.

Stories Should Reach the Heart

Making the case for change strictly using logic may move an audience toward acceptance; however, the necessary change will only be embraced if peoples' hearts are also won. Without question, one of the most effective ways to accomplish this is the use of stories.

Why are stories so effective? To begin with, listeners tend to lower their intellectual defenses. Stories are not generally perceived to be threatening.

Stories are also effective because listeners join in the creative process. Based on personal experiences, they create images in their minds that include more detail than the speaker is actually giving. This co-creation results in a sense of ownership. For the leader sharing a vision, this is invaluable -- it takes the vision from just being his or hers, to being "ours."

What Does the Audience Think?

"Leadership is a dialogue, not a monologue." -- *The Leadership Challenge* (Kouzes & Posner)

Whenever appropriate, a leader should be open to

questions and comments from the audience. This willingness to listen, and not just talk, both projects and inspires confidence. It also encourages the audience to further take ownership of the message.

It's Not Over Without a Call to Action

The final step in a leader's speech must be a specific and personal call to action. Once the story of change has been delivered and defended, it's time to tell the audience members what they should do to make it happen.

Tell the story of change, and then call for an active participation in it.

What will be derived from all these focused efforts? A successful leadership message that achieves lasting results.

William R. Steele is a senior training associate at BRODY Professional Development. He facilitates training programs and executive coaching sessions in presentation skills and effective meetings. He developed the "Speaking to Lead" course for BRODY. Bill can be contacted at 800-726-7936.

Why Use Humor in a Presentation?
by Tom Antion

"Why should I bother using humor in my presentations? Can't I just deliver my information and sit down?"

Yes, you sure can, and that's what most people do. The problem is that most people are not effective presenters. They are snooze-inducing, say-your-prayers, hit-the-sack, unlicensed hypnotists. They might be experts in their fields and be able to recite hours and hours of information on their topics, but is that effective? No. An effective presentation is one that achieves its purpose, whatever that may be.

I don't think that many presenters define their purpose clearly even to themselves. As part of being a strong presenter you must ask yourself: Why am I here? What do I want to accomplish? Am I here to sell something? Am I here to motivate? Am I here to persuade? Am I here to get votes? What do I want the audience members to take home with them when I'm done? Once you've answered these questions, I can tell you how and why humor can help you achieve your goals.

According to Bob Orben, special assistant to former President Gerald Ford and former director of the White House Speech Writing Department, "Business executives and political leaders have embraced humor because humor works. Humor has gone from being an admirable part of a leader's character to a mandatory one."

There is a higher level of professional speaker to progress to, and developing outstanding presentation skills will help you become that person.

A survey conducted by a large executive search firm of top executives who earned more than $250,000 per year, found that these executives believed their communication skills were the number one factor that carried them to the top. Mastering the use of humor and other high-explosion techniques puts a fine polish on those skills, which can help propel you to the top more quickly.

Like other top presenters, there are many benefits you can derive from using humor in your presentations. Keep in mind that these benefits only help you reach your ultimate purpose for making the presentation. They are not purposes themselves unless, of course, you are only interested in entertaining.

Using humor does the following for you:

HELPS YOU CONNECT WITH THE AUDIENCE. What audience is going to listen to you if its members don't feel you are one of them?

MAKES YOU MORE LIKEABLE. The more an audience likes you, the more its members will be likely to agree with your ideas.

AROUSES INTEREST. Many of you speak to audience members that don't even want to be there. Humor can help you gain their interest.

KEEPS ATTENTION. Grabbing interest at the beginning of a presentation is not enough to carry you to the end. You must keep the attention of the audience all the way. Unfortunately our audience's attention spans are becoming shorter and shorter. According to Ron Hoff in his presentation skills book *I Can See You Naked*, "If corporate managers ever saw their own meetings on TV, they would pick up their remote controls and zap themselves into oblivion in the flick of an eyelash." We are competing with movies that have $100 million in special effects. We must be prepared to deliver a fast-paced program that surprises members of the audience. At times we need to quickly capture their attention, and make sure they are listening to us. Humor will help you do this.

HELPS TO EMPHASIZE POINTS AND IDEAS. Anyone who has ever taken a basic speech course knows that you must hit audience members on the head with your point over and over before they get it. Humor is one of the hammers you can use.

DISARMS HOSTILITY. Nonfrivolous humor can be used to take the edge off audiences that are clearly against you.

REDUCES RELATIVE STATUS. Some of you are what I call the "big-shots" of your organization. Your position as boss creates a big barrier to listening. Making a little fun of yourself (self-effacing humor) will do wonders for opening lines of communication.

OVERCOMES OVERLY FLATTERING INTRO-DUCTIONS. Introducers come in all levels of quality. If you get one that makes you sound too good to be true, it will create expectations in the audience that you couldn't possibly live up to. Humor can neutralize this problem instantly.

GETS YOUR POINT ACROSS WITHOUT CRE-ATING HOSTILITY. Sometimes you have to deliver tough negative messages. The careful use of humor can help you do your dastardly deed without creating unnecessary anger.

HELPS RELATE FACTS AND FIGURES. A friend of mine likes to say, "I don't want to bore you with sadistics." Technical and financial presenters must be especially careful to spice up long lists of numbers and generally dry material. You must keep in mind that most people in your audience are not as passionate about your subject as you are, or they would be up in front of the group. Think from the audience's point of view, and do whatever it takes to break up boring material so you don't lose your audience totally.

Joan Eisenstodt, a former MPI Meeting Planner of the Year, says, "High content, informational speakers almost always fall flat if they don't use some humor. I equate appropriate humor with warmth, and audiences respond to warmth." She also notes, "After more than 25 years watching audiences and presenters, I know that even subtle humor can help the audience respond positively to information that could be considered boring."

MAKES A POSITIVE IMPRESSION. Laughter and good humor create bonds. Even if the audience members don't like you, they will like you better if you can make them laugh or smile and they will leave with better thoughts of you.

SHOWS THAT YOU DON'T TAKE YOURSELF TOO SERIOUSLY. The old saying goes, "If you take yourself too seriously, no one else will." If you can laugh a little bit at yourself at the right times, your audience can laugh with you and not at you.

HELPS PAINT PICTURES IN THE AUDIENCE'S MIND. The pictures humorous storytellers can paint are what people remember, not the words.

MAKES INFORMATION MORE MEMORABLE. Joyce Saltman, a college professor and well-known speaker in the health care field, did exhaustive research for her 1995 doctoral dissertation "Humor in Adult Learning." She concluded, "Most researchers agreed that humor generally aided in the retention of materials as well as to the enjoyment of the presentation of the information."

LIGHTENS UP HEAVY MATERIAL. Appropriate humor added to heavy, serious material gives the audience a few seconds to relax. Even Shakespeare employed this device, called "comic relief," extensively to provide distraction or offer respite from the serious events of a tragedy.

Here's my personal, experience-based list of *what humor can do for you:*

You probably will be asked back. If you succced in your original purpose, you may be asked back. If you also make audience members feel really good by entertaining them at the same time, your chances of being asked back will be much higher.

You will get higher marks on evaluations or more sales. If you make listeners feel good, they will like you better and reflect that in your evaluation scores or increased product sales.

You will make more money. If you are a professional presenter, you will be booked more and your fees will rise. If you present as part of your job, then read the next item carefully.

You will be more promotable. Having and conveying a sense of humor is on virtually everyone's list of top leadership skills. A humorous and engaging presentation style will push you up the ladder where good communications skills are a must.

If it's good enough for popes and presidents, it's good enough for you. I don't know about the pope, but I do know that all modern-day presidents are coached extensively on the use of appropriate humor for many of the reasons stated above.

You will make people happy. This is my favorite benefit. I get great satisfaction from knowing that I have brightened someone else's life. I had an executive come up to me after one of my humor seminars and say, "You opened up a whole new world for me." I almost cried right on the spot. I'll never forget it.

Tom Antion is a lively and entertaining keynote speaker and seminar leader. He is an expert in advanced presentation skills, speaking for money and small business Internet marketing. This segment is an excerpt from Tom's book WAKE 'EM UP Business Presentations *(Anchor Publishing). Tom can be reached at 800-448-6280, or e-mail orders@antion.com. You can get his free "Great Speaking" E-magazine at www.antion.com/ezinesubscribe.htm. Visit Tom's blog at www.GreatPublicSpeaking.BlogSpot.com.*

The Master of Ceremonies
by Ty Boyd, CSP, CPAE

This is an area where my expertise rivals just about anyone but Bob Barker or Pat Sajak.

Though I have always really enjoyed the emcee role, I never dreamed it would be such a big part of my work. Years of broadcasts, hundreds of pageants, fairs, award ceremonies of every description, the annual International Retailer of the Year Awards in Chicago, the Positive Thinking Rallies, not to mention more than 18 years at the CPAE Banquet at National Speakers Association, have all sharpened my ax.

What I've Learned

There are 12 things I have learned over the years:

1. **As emcee, you are the captain of the ship, the host.** The members of the audience are your guests. Your job is to make them comfortable, to create a dialogue between them and the various events on the program.
2. **The job calls for a sense of theater.**
3. **You are not the show, but you are responsible for the flow, the housekeeping, often the introductions, and the audience's concerns -- the total program.**
4. **You are not the star, but are still critical to the program's success.**
5. **This job requires preparation.** Do your homework.
6. **Either carry survival tools or know where to find them** (flashlight, extra script, filler

materials, etc.).

7. **You are the fire marshal.**
8. **It's your attitude that shows.**
9. **Set the stage for real people and a worthy audience.** Answer the audience's question of, "What's in it for me?"
10. **You are the sergeant-at-arms.**
11. **Have fun.**
12. **Don't overstep your boundaries.**

You can create a useful talent to enhance your value to the meeting professional. Work hard enough that the meeting planner will want you to return as the emcee next year. Then you can sell a speech to go with it!

The Introducer

Too few people are introduced effectively. I always advise speakers to write their own intros. It's sometimes the only commercial you will get. Additionally, I instruct them to print reading instructions on the page with the intro. Simply say, "Please read as written." Funny thing, when we have that instruction on the intro, people will work so much harder to do it well – and just the way you have written it. It beats some clown saying, "Well, here's an old buddy-buddy of mine. Never dreamed we'd be paying him to tell us anything about this subject. Let's give a warm welcome to this fool!"

Being the introducer requires that we create an atmosphere of mutual respect between the audience and the speaker. We need to answer several questions: Why this speaker? At this time? For this audience and at this place? As a speaker, you know how much better the event goes when these questions are answered.

Here are some pointers to remember when introducing others:

- You are the stage setter.
- Create an inviting environment.
- Do your homework.
- Be really interested in the speaker and subject. Show it.
- Unless the speaker is a celebrity, use his or her name several times. Audiences forget.
- Be a little bit on the gossipy side. Make the introduction sound like a novel not a textbook. Be sure to answer the audience's unasked question, "What's in it for me?"
- Never introduce a female as "Mrs. John Smith" or in a sexist way.
- When you make an introduction, speak to the audience, not to the person being introduced.
- Do not upstage or over praise.
- While you are on stage, you are the captain of the ship. Don't leave the center spot until the speaker has arrived. Welcome the speaker with a handshake, nod, smile or slight touch on the

shoulder, then exit. It's now his or her show.

- Model good listening.
- Lead the applause. Model the behavior you would expect from the audience.

You may not be compensated for simply introducing a speaker, but the more proficiency you display on the platform, the more desirable you become as a total package. Many times the roles of emcee and introducer are combined.

Ty Boyd is a speaker, author, and communications coach to thousands. He has won the three highest awards of the National Speakers Association. Ty is a member of both the Speakers and Broadcasters Hall of Fame. In 1980, Ty Boyd founded the Excellence in Speaking Institute (ESI). His latest book is The Million Dollar Toolbox, a Blueprint for Transforming Your Life and your Career with Powerful Presentation Skills. *Learn more at www.TyBoyd.com or by calling 800-336-2693.*

Voice Training: Who Needs It?

by Ralph E. Hillman, Ph.D.

"My voice is fine, thank you!" Speakers who say this often experience a variety of voice ailments: sore throats, "tired voices," hoarseness, loss of voice, excessive throat clearing, etc.

Speakers attribute these ailments to "fatigue" or "overuse" of their voices. In reality, our voices are not tired or over used, they are abused. How we speak when we are speaking is what hurts us. Most people who have these recurring vocal concerns often exhibit breathy characteristics as well as associated vocal fold tension which results in vocal abuse. Using a breathy voice is OK for emphasis or to soften the glottal attack on initial vowels. Speakers incur vocal ailments when they add excessive vocal tension to an already breathy vocal sound. The exaggerated example would be people shouting at a football game. Long before the second half, they are whispering because their voices are gone.

WHAT IS BREATHINESS?

During healthy sound production, the vocal folds are pulled together with just enough muscle tension to allow them to be forced apart by air pressure from the diaphragm. These vibrations occur very rapidly; 256 cycles per second for middle C.

The unhealthy habitually breathy voice quality is the result of the vocal folds opening too widely and often not making complete closure with each cycle and thus allowing excessive air to pass between the folds. In the attempt to make complete closure, additional muscle tension is required, making the vocal folds slam together during each cycle.

Because you are most likely breathy, in habitual sound

production, when you use the tense voice quality, you sound different to yourself than you do to others. We hear ourselves primarily as the sound is transmitted from our vocal folds, through bone, cartilage and tissue to our ears. Others hear us with the sound going through the air and then to the ears. Professionals often do not know they are being breathy, because they have not learned to hear it. In addition, breathiness makes the presence of other voice qualities, that is, nasal or muffled, almost impossible to distinguish.

WHAT CAUSES BREATHINESS?

Basically, there are three conditions which prevent the vocal folds from making complete closure and are responsible for the breathy symptoms.

1. The lack of appropriate muscle tension in the vocal folds. These are learned habit patterns which are deeply ingrained in the muscle reflexes themselves. Since speech production is a learned skill, the habit of keeping the muscles of the vocal folds too loose during speech production can be changed. You can voluntarily control that pattern by using a more tense voice quality; cutting down on the amount of air exhaled during speech.

2. The lack of sufficient muscle tension around the back of the posterior end of the vocal folds, (the oblique & transverse arytenoid muscles, that pull the arytenoid cartilages and the posterior ends of the vocal folds together), **resulting in an interarytenoid notch or vocal "chink" at the posterior end of the vocal folds.** This chink, or space, allows air to pass between the folds before, during and after speech production, regardless of the tension of the muscles of the vocal folds. These muscles can be strengthened with the trill/swallow exercise.

3. The presence of a polyp, nodule, carcinoma or some other pathology which prevents the vocal folds from adducting or coming together. These are often the result of improper functioning of the vocal folds. Consult an ear, nose, and throat specialist (sometimes abbreviated ENT or more precisely identified as an otolaryngologist), if you suspect you might have a problem you are not able to change or correct using the suggestions found here.

WHERE DO I BEGIN?

For the first step, let us look at the standard assumptions regarding our general physical health. Since each of them can have an effect on speech production, most people need to heed these before starting voice training. These assumptions will not be detailed here, because they really are self explanatory. If you do have questions regarding these assumptions, contact me directly.

• **Eat right before speaking.** Avoid milk and other dairy products, chocolate, soft drinks/sweeteners and sugar, or any foods which you know thicken the saliva in your mouth. Help your voice and body as a whole to stay healthy.

• **Drink water, eight glasses a day,** to cleanse the body and keep the vocal folds moist.

• **Use Entertainer's Secret, a great nose and throat moisturizer** to lubricate and open up your nose and throat.

• **Do weekly aerobic exercise.** Doing a daily routine to keep your heart healthy and your muscles limber.

• **Get adequate sleep, maintaining consistent body clock hours** (getting up and going to bed at the same time).

• **Minimize exposure to dust, smoke, and noise.**

• **Avoid alcohol and recreational drugs,** and **follow the advice of health care professionals before taking any medications.** If you have diabetes, asthma, high blood pressure, clinical depression, etc., you can't avoid drugs. Just be careful to avoid abusing them.

• **Keep a positive focus.** Maintain a positive attitude and work at smiling, which releases healing endorphins.

Utilizing these suggestions will help make sure your

body is healthy and ready for you when you need to speak effectively.

What? I Need to Work on Posture, Neck & Shoulder Muscle Tension and My Breathing?

The second step calls for mastering the "Big Three." Mastery of these three separate physical areas will not guarantee you "perfect" speech, but most people can hear a difference in the improved sound.

A) Posture or Stance

The six essentials for good posture:

- Unlock your knees while standing. OK, you knew that. Locking your knees cuts off the blood flow to your brain. Ever watch people who are standing at attention pass out?

- Keep your pelvis level, not too far forward or back.

- Tuck your tummy, keeping it firm from the belly-button down.

- Raise your rib cage; be able to feel the bottoms of your ribs all the time, not just while speaking.
- Keep your shoulders back and down. It will look and feel military.

- Keep your head up on top. A straight line goes from

the top of your ear to the top of your shoulder,
to the top of your hip to the center of your foot.

A lifetime activity of good posture needs to be checked at least once an hour, for every hour you are awake, for the rest of your life. Make the commitment! Check your posture with your body parallel to a wall. If your head is well forward of the perpendicular line of the wall, or your shoulders are rolled forward, or your rib cage is down, or your pelvis is tipped, the following are likely to be affected or result:

1. the flow of oxygen-rich blood to your brain
2. restricted breathing
3. tongue pulled back, making clear diction difficult
4. elevated pitch-muscles of the larynx are tight and the vocal folds are not free to move
5. arytenoids pulled apart, imposing a breathy sound, allowing air to pass even when it is unintended
6. muscles of the larynx affecting tense or relaxed vocal fold closure.
Thus, your posture can effect the breathiness of your vocal production.

Do this exercise: Put your hands (palms forward) up and back against the wall at shoulder height (in the "I give up" position). Placing a "Hillman Handle" (a broom handle) in back of your shoulder blades with the wrists of your hands in back of that handle can help you position the shoulders. Now the "I give up" position can become a reality. Keep your head up on top and elevate your rib cage. If you can not hold that position for any length of time, your shoulders have been pulled forward for too long. Over time, pulling your shoulders back and straightening your spine down will relax your whole body. Now try counting to five. Contrast that count to five with a count when you are using your old posture. You should sound much louder and clearer when up against the wall. Ultimately, this posture allows the larynx to be free of excessive external muscle tension that might restrict or inhibit efficient vocal fold movement.

If the military bearing of this posture activity may feel stiff and awkward, you are on the right track. You do not need to be rigid, but you do need to sit and stand with erect posture. The erect posture should be your "home" position. Be free to move around, but when you are finished moving, return to the "home" position. Check yourself in the mirror or record yourself on video. Ask friends and family how you and your new posture look to them. Some will complain that you look stiff and vigilant. Thank them for noticing. One must practice this response. Otherwise, we tend to apologize and effort at good posture is extinguished. Most of them will prefer the more alert and attentive bearing of your body. Soon your face will reflect the relaxed condition of the rest of your body.

Those who make a consistent attempt to maintain their new posture often begin to experience a self-concept shift. Most people feel more positive about themselves and more in control of who they are -- especially on the platform.

B) Neck and Shoulder Muscles

Avoid tension of the muscles on the front and sides of your neck, for any reason. Even though our posture is straightened, and we should be physically relaxed, it is very possible for us to keep our neck and shoulder muscles in a tense condition. Many speakers persist in staying in this condition, because often they are not aware the condition exists; or they believe those behaviors indicate emotional interest in the audience they are addressing.

Although easily overlooked, detection of tense neck and shoulder muscles is crucial. Besides, tightening the neck muscles and/or thrusting your head forward as a result is ugly. Put your hand to your neck to feel the tension while breathing and speaking, or watch for tension in a mirror or on video. When the neck and shoulder muscles are tight, the muscle movement in and around the larynx is inhibited. This phenomenon directly impacts the quality of the sound of your voice.

C) Breath Support

Diaphragmatic breathing involves using the muscles of the diaphragm which attach at the base of the rib cage and hump up into the chest cavity. When breathing most efficiently, the muscle activity and movement will be around the torso between the bellybutton and the base of the sternum. The ribs should move sideways. Keep the tummy firm from the bellybutton down, expanding the rib cage sideways using the upper abdominal muscles without raising the shoulders or puffing out the lower abdominal cavity (our lungs are not down there).

To obtain the most value from diaphragmatic breathing utilize a "Cleansing Breath," which really can be a valuable stress reduction tool. Dr. Richard Quisling a practicing Otolaryngolist in Hermitage, Tennessee, calls this a Cleansing Breath because it provides the lungs and your body with the cleansing effect of more oxygen.

Performing a Cleansing Breath is simple: Keeping your posture erect (using the steps to good posture and keeping the head up with shoulders back and down), relax your neck and shoulder muscles completely, which fills the lungs, allowing the air to enter through your nose freely and easily. Now, completely empty your lungs BY FORCING THE AIR OUT, by blowing through pursed lips, under pressure using your diaphragm. To know that you are getting the full benefit of a Cleansing Breath, place your hands around your abdominal area at your sides. You should feel this area moving in and out, expanding sideways. Now repeat. A Cleansing Breath will relax your spirit, voice and body. While you are doing the lifetime hourly posture routine, practice doing Cleansing Breaths.

Breathing Contrast Exercise: Test the impact of the oxygen exchange when doing a Cleansing Breath. Do four Cleansing Breaths in a row with the lip constriction and lots of air pressure from the diaphragm (lower thoracic/upper abdominal area). After you have done the four Cleansing Breaths, note the strong possibility that you are experiencing a head rush. Now, for contrast, using the Big Three, fill your lungs and gently release the air with no constrictions and minimal air pressure. No head rush! By forcing out the air, you are encouraging a greater oxygen exchange in your lungs and getting more oxygen into your blood. That oxygen-rich blood is spread throughout your body, and some of it actually makes its way to your brain. The benefits of additional oxygen in your brain should be obvious. Regular Cleansing Breaths strengthen the diaphragm muscles, providing more breath support for speech.

What Can I Do to Hear Breathiness?

The third step is to listen to other people in whom the breathiness is obvious. It is easier to hear breathiness in others. You also might want to note the values you attach to the personalities of those who habitually use the breathy voice quality. Typical stereotypes of habitually breathy speakers include weak, passive or sexy. As speakers we need to occasionally use the breathy voice quality for emphasis to indicate those qualities as perceived, as well as being soft and gentle or compassionate. Learning more about the stereotypes associated with voice qualities is an interesting study; but that is another article.

To hear breathiness in yourself do the Breathy Contrast exercise: Try counting aloud from three to nine, exhaling lots of air as you count. Use the flat of your hand in front of your mouth to feel the amount of air being expelled. The vocal folds are trying to operate efficiently by making complete closure during each cycle, but they are unable to do so because of the lack of appropriate vocal fold tension which would restrict the air flow.

Now, contrast the breathy voice quality with the production of a much more tense sound. In a rather staccato fashion, cutting off the end of the sound of each word, do the count again. You should sound louder and feel less air passing out of your mouth and hitting your hand as you count. Do this negative practice, exaggerating both conditions. Once you are aware of the differences, you may choose to use varying degrees of breathiness anywhere along the continuum.

Standing push-up exercise: With your feet 18 to 24 inches from the wall, your hands on the wall at shoulder level, say "ah" as you let your rigid body lean toward the wall, bending only at your ankles. When your head is a few inches from the wall, stop the forward movement and stop the sound. You should hear and feel the vocal folds close. As you approach the wall, you should hear the breathiness diminish. Now try to mimic that closure without doing the push-up. Being aware of the sound of breathiness will be enough to diminish its use.

What Exercises Will Help Me Change My Breathy Habit?

Trill/Swallow exercise: Strengthen the muscles holding the arytenoids together.

1. Trill/Swallow

a) With good posture, relaxed neck & shoulders, and efficient breath support, initiate a cleansing breath (fill your lungs).
b) Elevate your chin toward the ceiling.
c) Trill your tongue off the alveolar ridge (or rapidly tap your tongue off the gum ridge behind your upper front teeth).
d) Hum, going up in pitch.
e) When you hit your highest pitch, swallow (if you can't swallow, lower your chin slightly and try again).
f) Keeping your chin elevated, restart the trill, coming down in pitch to your lowest pitch.
g) Do another cleansing breath.

2. Echo
Reduce breathiness by producing an echo off a wall, to make vocal fold movement more efficient. This is not a volume exercise. This exercise can also be done by

bouncing the sound off the windshield of a car. If you do not hear an echo, you are probably being too breathy.

If you must persist in being habitually breathy, the least you can do is avoid glottal attacks. Glottal attacks occur primarily on vowels which are the first voiced sounds of words. The vocal folds are brought together quickly and with excessive pressure to make the sound sharp and clear. You can avoid this vocal abuse by connecting these initial vowel sounds to the last sound of the previous word. So avoid "punching" or stressing words that begin with a vowel.

Even though you may not think you need voice training, and you are not experiencing vocal discomfort, EVERY TIME BEFORE YOU SPEAK do a voice warm-up. Voice warm-up: Be sure the "Big Three" are in place. Hum at optimum pitch (four to eight pitches up from your lowest pitch), and at a soft volume. Resist breathiness. Then hum, expanding the range slowly up and down the scale as you get louder. Take at least five minutes.

Awareness is the key. Take full advantage of this breathiness information by doing the contrast practice, so you can learn to hear it. Listen, as you practice to control it. Remember, there is nothing wrong with being breathy, just do not add the tense voice quality to it. Speakers can use breathiness to their advantage only if they know how to control it.

Ralph E. Hillman, Ph.D. – The Speaker Who Speaks With Speakers about Speaking, Mentoring Speakers to Improve Their Credibility, Using BREATHE to Stay on Goal and Maintain Control, author of Communication Strategies, Work for Your Voice, *and* Delivering Dynamic Presentations: Using Your Voice and Body for Impact *(published by Allyn & Bacon) – is a keynote speaker and speaking coach, and former college professor. Call 615-482-3117, or e-mail Ralph@TheBreatheSystem.com, or visit www.TheBreatheSystem.com*

Six Principles of Audience-Centered Seating™
by Paul O. Radde, Ph.D.

Proper room arrangements can positively impact the audience's ability to bond, the interaction of a group, and its response to the speaker.

Here are **six basic principles for planning and troubleshooting any presentation setup**:

1) Set the room toward the long wall, so that participants can be closer to the presenter and facilitators. This makes the exchange more inclusive and personal. Those in front can be more intimate. Those in the back are still closer than they would be in a bowling alley setup facing the narrow wall.

2) Curve the seating -- no straight rows. Curved rows promote learning, comfort, safety, networking, bonding, line of sight and capacity. If you will entertain a group discussion or problem-solving session, place the group in a semicircle facing visual surfaces such as a screen or flip charts. When you can occupy the open area in the middle, you can step in front should one member verbally attack another, then, redirect group attention and energy back to the agenda item, problem, or issue at hand.

3) Flare the aisles out 45 degrees from the corner of the platform toward the exits -- no center aisle. Aisles flared out toward the exits provide greater carrying capacity and traffic, especially at the exit doors where traffic is heaviest. Plus, those entering and exiting on an aisle acting as a radius of a circle, blocks no one's view of the presentation.

4) Face each chair directly toward the presentation. The most symmetrical room setup may appear to be neat and orderly, but it may wreak havoc on the spines of those seated. Facing each chair may not look as neat, but it functions to provide maximum comfort and line of sight for the participant.

5) Cut single-chair width access lanes into the larger seating sections. This ensures ease of access to chairs. Latecomers will tend to stand in the back rather than cross over in front of several seated participants to get to a middle seat. Access lanes increase the number of easy access seats, and aid traffic flow, getting participants in and out faster during breaks to keep the meeting on schedule.

6) In crowded, smaller meeting rooms, set the back row along the back wall. Leave an aisle in front of the back row, which is more likely to stay unimpeded in the event of an emergency exit. If the room is really crowded, and cannot accommodate everyone seated, then leave the back of the room open for a greater number to stand. Move the water table out into the hall to clear more space.

Remember to light the faces of those who will address the group. Many audience members have impaired hearing and read lips to fully understand. They may not even be aware of this fact. However, if they can't see you, they can't hear you. And the misunderstanding or failure to keep up with exchanges can muddle the meeting. Lighting the face of a speaker is really essential, but curiously enough, is often overlooked.

Dr. Paul O. Radde is the author of Savvy Seating: Get Your Audience the Best Seats in the House ... and Increase Capacity, *as well as* Thrival! A Little Taste of Heaven on Earth, *which is the title of his keynote address. Contact: Paul@Thrival.com, (303) 818-8795, or through http://www.Thrival.com*

Power, Punch and Pizzazz
by Ray Pelletier, CSP, CPAE

Whoever you are ... whatever your particular style ... whatever the subject ... whatever the makeup of your audience ... there are several fundamentals to keep in mind when designing a motivational presentation.

The first and foremost is to develop a solid mindset that you are there to meet the needs of your audience. This is more than just something you tell yourself; it has to be YOUR motivation for being there in the first place. And it has to show -- it has to be perfectly obvious to everyone in the room. The old axiom is a fact: Nobody cares how much you know until they know how much you care. Unless you are motivated by that great truth, and believe and practice it thoroughly, I suggest you change your line of work; you're unlikely to serve your client properly or to motivate any audience.

With the audience's needs in mind, pre-program research becomes essential. The client can give you a summation of the problems that need to be solved, but it is up to you to conduct your own research into the audience attitudes and feelings you'll be encountering. This is the only way you'll know how to relate to your listeners and reach them on a personal level where you can accomplish what the client has asked of you. (As professional speaker Phil Wexler put it, "Prescription without diagnosis is malpractice.").

I've carried out pre-program research in a number of ways. One way is through questionnaires to prospective audience members (the list being supplied by the Meeting Planner). I assure confidentiality and ask recipients of the questionnaire for their views about such subjects as competition, product quality/service, marketing, teamwork, corporate communication and their general feelings about the company and their job and whatever problems they may be having. It's amazing what you can learn about the corporate culture from such a questionnaire -- it can sometimes be very different from the snapshot you get from a Meeting Planner.

But by far the most productive research method is to arrange for casual, one-on-one interviews with several prospective members of the audience at some point before the seminar. Face-to-face meetings enable you to sense nuances that won't be obvious in the written answers to a questionnaire. An added benefit of personal interviews is that you'll be able to look out at your audience during a seminar and see people you've met and whose attitudes and feelings you know. You'll better understand how to reach them. And if your several interviewees are reasonably representative of the audience as a whole (almost invariably the case), you'll have found the hot buttons that can reach and motivate most, if not all, of your listeners. They'll have no doubt that you're speaking to THEM, with THEIR needs in mind. They'll be surprised. They'll find it refreshing. They'll respect you. And they will listen.

The meeting ENVIRONMENT is another matter you should attend to with great care. That it should be friendly, welcoming and positive goes without saying. But it is also extremely important that the meeting room, and the way it is set up, reflects your message in an exciting and entertaining way. In my case, it isn't unusual to see signage all over the walls, as well as bullet-point placards that will reinforce my message as I go along. Props, such as ladders, chairs, luggage and other odd items that will be used to animate and illustrate segments of my message are often in full view on and off stage. People see all of this as they come into the room. They wonder about it. They're curious. There's an excitement about it. It puts them in an expectant mood. They're here for a real show. It's fun.

Well-chosen props are learning and remembrance aids that invariably drive home a point far more dramatically than words alone. If it's not your habit to use them, I suggest you experiment a little bit. Just try it. Even the most serious and somber seminar can benefit from a choice prop or two. Props bring words to life. I also often include music and video clips in that mix. Audience involvement and participation is another of the fundamental points motivational speakers will be wise to keep in mind. The more audience members are involved in a presentation, the more they'll enjoy and remember it.

SPEAKING STYLE, of course, is a matter of individual taste and purpose, and I won't presume to suggest one. But here, again, a common advantage is available to any speaker who can sprinkle selected anecdotes and parables throughout their message. This is a tried, true and much-honored method of adding flavor and understanding to any subject -- from the most light-hearted anecdote to the most serious and profound story.

Simplicity and clarity are also common fundamentals ... the real "master-keys" to effective communicating. Before I walk onto a platform, I invariably remind myself of this: KISS -- Keep It Simple, Simon! This is not a sign of disrespect toward an audience. It is a sign of the very highest respect. I have no intention of confusing an audience and wasting the time of a few hundred people who are just as bright, perceptive and smart as I am. They deserve a nonambiguous message that can be understood immediately. Crafting that kind of message – going over it again and again with an eye to absolute clarity – is an essential discipline, no matter what your speaking style may be.

Sometimes, in my seminars, I ask everybody to start conversing with the people beside them in language geared to 8-year-olds. No big words. Just childhood language.

They love it! The energy is really high in the room. But, most importantly, audience members learn that when they speak as simply as possible there is never any confusion about what is being said. Everyone understands everyone else.

Here they are, all grown-up and sophisticated -- and yet the best way to be sure they're understood by everyone at all times is to speak in the simple, nonambiguous language of childhood!

The real bottom line to successful motivational speaking can probably be summed up this way: The privilege of the platform is to be taken literally. It is a privilege – and a great responsibility – to mold and motivate an audience. If you consistently bear that in mind, you can't help but be audience-oriented, and you will instinctively come to understand the basics that are necessary for success – the fundamentals that are necessary for you to put on a memorable program with power, punch and pizzazz.

It all comes down to being there for THEM, not for yourself. All audience members in the world know the difference -- and, I promise you, they will respond accordingly.

Ray Pelletier, CSP, CPAE Speakers Hall of Fame -- was known as "America's Leadership Advisor" -- and was an international keynoter, seminar leader and management consultant. Ray passed away in 2005, but his legacy lives on. Expansion on the material in this article can be found in his book, Thanks Coach! *(Oakhill Press). Or, visit www.RayPelletier.com.*

Selling as a Life Skill
by Tim Connor, CSP

Many people only look at selling as selling products or services. In this section, we will look at the concept of selling as the ability to influence and persuade people. Everyone sells or doesn't sell every day. Parents sell values, morals and ethics, teachers sell study habits and learning as a lifelong process, politicians sell their ideas or platforms, managers sell policies and procedures, and children sell 24 hours a day for the better part of their early lives. They do not sell a product or service, have never attended a sales seminar or read a book on sales, but can they ever sell. I will bet wherever you live, there are several hundred people who will apply for new positions today. Most will have the experience, talent and qualifications, but will not be selected because they lack the ability to sell themselves.

Getting a good seat in a restaurant, asking your boss for a raise, and everything else in life, requires this vital ability. You either get what you want in life, or you don't. Most of the people who don't, lack the ability to influence and persuade others.

Let's discuss the attitude concepts, behaviors and skills that people who get what they want effectively use.

Attitude concepts

There are several concepts that impact your ability to successfully influence and persuade people. The most important ones are: self-image, self-confidence, self-worth, your goals and your ability to effectively communicate.

Self-image is how you feel about yourself. If you don't like yourself, it will be difficult to convince others that you deserve what it is you are trying to sell or get. Self-confidence is having the attitude that you can successfully handle whatever comes your way regardless of obstacles, difficulty or circumstances. You trust yourself. Self-worth is when you value what you know, can do and believe in, regardless of the opinions, actions or feelings of others. Your goals are the direction in life you are traveling. Clear goals contribute to your ability to see into the future with hope, vision, passion and purpose. Your ability to communicate effectively is a function of your vocabulary, desire to express your thoughts clearly, your willingness to listen and understand, and the courage to say what you mean and mean what you say.

These attitude concepts dramatically influence your ability to effectively persuade others. Without them, it will be difficult to achieve any real power. (I am using power as your ability to have congruence between your values, beliefs, thoughts and actions).

Behaviors

Behavior is how you act out daily -- your purpose and goals, or lack of them, your inner feeling and attitudes, and your beliefs and values. Personality is one way we define ourselves to the surrounding world. Are you sending a clear message that you know what you want, have the ability to get it and will pursue it until you are successful, or are you sending the message that you are a victim and not worthy of other people's attention, time, energy and interest?

Ever notice how some people achieve greater life success than others? Want to know the common denominator in every case where this is true? I have been discussing it for several minutes. It is their ability to influence and persuade others; to sell themselves, their ideas, their products, their needs and desires.

Skills

Now that we have briefly set the stage, let's discuss a few practical tips that can improve your ability in this critical area of life. We'll break these skills into five major areas:

a) the ability to get information
b) the ability to see clearly (to manage your perceptions)
c) the ability to give information that is consistent with your intent
d) the ability to ensure that the other party or parties have understood your meaning and intent
e) and a clear awareness of your objectives.

The ability to get information

The person that asks the questions controls the conversation, the person who talks the most dominates it. The key to gaining influence is not what you say, but what you know. The use of information is power. Questions are the best way to get information. There are two major types of questions; open and closed. Open questions ask for feelings, attitudes, opinions and general information. Closed questions ask for a yes or no or a specific fact. Closed questions shut down further dialogue, and open questions encourage more response. The key to getting information, so that you can decide what information is useful to use, is to ask more open than closed questions.

The ability to see clearly

Life is a perceptual experience. No one looks at life and its circumstances the same. This gives life its color, uniqueness and diversity as well as a great deal of frustration, conflict and misunderstanding. To see life from another person's perspective requires a lot of insight, flexibility, ego control, compassion and emotional maturity.

To see life as it really is requires that you remain open to change, receptive to other points of view and that you let go of old emotional baggage and attachments. It also requires that you let go of future attachments to outcomes of certain events and people. Neither of these are easy to accomplish, but are necessary to see life as it really is, not as you would like it to be.

The ability to give information

The tools we use to send information are verbal and

nonverbal messages. Verbal messages represent a small portion of the overall communication message. If there is an inconsistency between the words and the nonverbal signals you send, you will confuse the other person. Also, if you are receiving mixed signals, both verbal and nonverbal, the nonverbal will always be more accurate. This is primarily true because nonverbal signals come from a person's unconscious mind, and are not within his or her conscious control. Yes, we can send dedicated, conscious nonverbal signals when we are trying to send a particular message to another person, but these happen less than the natural, unconscious signals.

The verbal method of sending information is with words. The purpose of a good vocabulary is to give you flexibility with your choice of words. A good vocabulary is one of the most important skills to develop to improve your ability to influence and persuade. Without a good vocabulary, you will find yourself limited in your use of appropriate or persuasive language. However, remember the purpose of communication is to express yourself, not impress people. Don't use big words if a smaller one will get the job done.

The ability to ensure understanding

I will guarantee that in the past 48 hours, you have had a misunderstanding with someone. I will bet it was due to one of the following causes: assumptions were made, expectations were not communicated, the pace of the delivery was faster or slower than you are comfortable with, there were hidden agendas, or it was poor listening habits by you or the other party or parties.

A clear awareness of your objectives

If a ship doesn't reach the harbor, it isn't the harbor's fault. To get what you want, you have to know what you want. This, at first glance, might seem to be a simplistic cliché. However, after more than 30 years in sales and 20 years teaching selling, it is my conclusion that most people just wing their way through life, hoping that what they want will magically come to them without any clear objectives, plan or action.

A general goal will tend to give you general behavior, therefore general results. Specific goals will give you specific behavior and give you more specific results.

Let's wrap it up

To successfully sell, influence and persuade people, it is necessary to communicate with clarity and focus, have confidence in your beliefs, values and life philosophy and know your objectives. And it is vital that you live with congruence and passion.

It is also critical that you understand that the principles used by today's top salespeople to sell their products and services are no different than the skills necessary to get your dream job or influence a group of people in a professional presentation.

Tim Connor, CSP, has been a full-time speaker and sales and management trainer since 1973. He is the author of 45 books, including Soft Sell, *now in its 65th printing,* The Male Gift Giving Survival Guide, The Last Goodbye, Nitpickers, Naggers & Tyrants, The Road to Happiness is Full of Potholes, *and* That's Life. *You can reach him at 704-895-1230, or visit him on the Internet: www.TimConnor.com, tim@TimConnor.com.*

Presentation Skills for Trainers
by Karen Lawson, Ph.D., CSP

Like it or not, trainers are also performers. It's becoming increasingly more difficult to gain and maintain program participants' attention and interest. Corporate classroom audiences expect and demand to be entertained as well as trained. They want the learning experience to be both meaningful and enjoyable. Although challenging, meeting these needs and expectations is not difficult if you incorporate interactive techniques in your training design.

Get Them Active From the Start

Participant involvement is critical to the success of your training program. "People learn by doing, not by being told," a basic principle of adult learning, should be your guide in designing any training program, from the highly technical to the so-called "soft skills" addressed in human resource development programs.

From the very beginning, participants need to be engaged. You can create immediate involvement with a variety of fun, yet content-related activities and techniques. Opening activities can accomplish several goals:

1. involving the participants immediately in the learning experience
2. creating a risk-free learning environment
3. communicating personal responsibility for learning
4. introducing the content
5. building group cohesiveness
6. assessing participant needs and expectations

Be sure to choose an opening activity that will accomplish several goals or objectives. For example, one very successful technique is called, "What Do You Want to Know?" You, the trainer, post flip chart pages on the wall, each with a heading that corresponds to the major topics of the training program. Then give a packet of Post-it® notes to all participants, and ask them to write down questions they have about any of the topics. They may fill as many notes as they want, but put only one question per note. The participants then get up and place their questions under the appropriate headings. You can then categorize the questions and compare them to the learning objectives of the session. This method gives participants an opportunity to express their expectations anonymously. They are also immediately engaged in the process, thinking about the content, and beginning to take ownership for their learning. The only goal this activity does not meet is building group cohesiveness.

Involving Your Audience

Group involvement, a critical component of an effective training session, is easy if you follow the principles and practices of cooperative or peer learning.

Cooperative learning is the instructional use of small groups so that participants work together to maximize their own and each other's learning. For our purpose, a small group can be as few as two people or as many as eight. As trainers, we need to keep two very important principles in mind:

1. learning by nature is an active endeavor
2. different people learn in different ways

With those principles in mind, trainers need to use a variety of methods that will ensure a high level of participation and a moderate level of content.

The trainer needs to create many opportunities for the participants to interact with each other. Often this may involve asking people to work in pairs to come up with a joint answer to a question posed by the trainer, prepare a list of guidelines related to the topic, or discuss individual responses. Pairs ensure 100 percent participant involvement in a low-risk environment.

The use of small groups is a very effective way to get people involved. Use small groups to generate ideas, discuss concepts, solve problems, or work on case studies. Small groups provide more opportunities for people to contribute and participate. Often, those who are reluctant to speak up in a large group situation seem to "come alive" when placed in a small group setting.

Interacting With the Audience

Many trainers use role playing as a skill-building technique in their training programs. More often than not, this technique does not achieve the desired results because of participant resistance.

One very effective, nonthreatening way of using role play is to conduct a demonstration role play. You would have prepared a scripted role play depicting either the right way or wrong way of using a particular skill, technique, or process. Early in the session, select two "actors" from the group, and give them the script so they will have an opportunity to familiarize themselves with their parts prior to the demonstration. At the appropriate point in the program, ask the "players" to come forward and simply read their scripts while the rest of the group observes the interaction for various do's and don'ts that illustrate the learning points.

Another nonthreatening role play technique involves the trainer as one of the role players. Ask for a volunteer to come up front and assume the role of the other person. For example, in a "Customer Service" session, you want to demonstrate how to deal with an irate customer. You assume the role of the customer service representative, and ask for a volunteer to play the irate customer who is returning a piece of merchandise for a full refund. The "employee" (played by the trainer) is not permitted to give a refund, only store credit. As the role play begins, the "customer" demands a refund. At this point, you stop the action and turn to the participants for coaching. When the action resumes, you as the employee follow the group's suggestions in responding to the customer. This stop-action technique is used several times throughout the role play.

Trainers who want to promote interaction will often use open-ended questions to encourage participation. Although this technique is useful, its biggest flaw is that generally a handful of people respond. Many trainers complain that the same people are answering all the questions or offering input. There are several techniques that will guarantee 100 percent audience response. One method is to use response cards. Hand each participant cards to use in responding to multiple choice (A, B, C, D) or true-false (T, F) questions. Develop three or four statements or questions to which participants will respond with their cards. As you read (or show) each item, participants will respond by holding up the card of their choice.

Another way to get every person to respond is to use an active response system. Choose four or five questions or statements designed to get participants to express their opinions about a certain topic. For example, to introduce the topic of "Managing Conflict," you might choose the following statements:

- Conflict is inevitable.
- Conflict increases during times of change.
- Conflict can lead to either creative or dysfunctional results.
- Conflict should be encouraged.

You would ask participants to stand. As you display the first statement, ask participants to remain standing if they agree with the statement, and sit down if they disagree. Then ask a few people to explain why they agreed or disagreed before moving on to the next statement. An alternative approach would be to ask participants to hold up cards with an "A" for agree and "D" for disagree.

Using Theatrical Techniques

It's show time! Each training session should be a carefully crafted and choreographed production, enhanced and enlivened by the use of theatrical techniques, including props, costumes, and staging. The idea is to make the training experience memorable.

A great way to start is to have a theme. For example, for a team-building session, you might choose a sports theme. Training materials would include sports graphics such as pictures of people playing sports and various sports equipment. To reinforce your message of the importance of creating a team environment, bring props to the session. Use a referee's whistle to bring the group back together at the end of a group activity. Use ball caps to indicate team leaders. When you break into subgroup activities, you could group people by different sports. For example, one group might be baseballs; another basketballs; and others could be footballs, soccer balls, tennis racquets, hockey sticks, etc. Pictures of these various pieces of sports equipment would indicate the location of each subgroup in the room or break-out rooms.

Or if you choose to use one sport as a central theme – let's say football – then each subgroup would be assigned the name of a professional football team. You could play recorded team "fight songs" to create the mood as participants enter the room or during breaks. To encourage participation, reward participants with "prizes" of sports paraphernalia such as mini sports balls, key chains, etc. You could also use sports items attached to cards listing key learning points as give-aways. These little reminders are powerful reinforcement tools. If you're really adventurous, you might even come to the session dressed as a referee, a football player or cheerleader. One thing's for sure – you'll get their attention!

If your comfort zone calls for the less dramatic, you can still use props as metaphors to make your point and reinforce the learning. For example, in a session on change, you might show a "Slinky" to illustrate the need for flexibility. The "Magic Eye" posters are a great way to show how we need to look beyond the obvious and see things differently. A compass can be used in a session on goal setting to represent the need for direction. The possibilities are endless, and you are bound only by your imagination.

Creating Word Pictures

Powerful presentation skills include the ability to create mental images, whether you're on the stage or in the classroom. Mental imagery or visualization can be very effective in helping participants create a picture in their minds and overcome obstacles. For example, in a "Presentation Skills" class, the trainer might use visualization to help participants overcome stage fright. You would start by playing relaxation music to create the mood. You would then ask participants to close their eyes, relax, and begin breathing deeply. Next, ask them to picture a favorite place where they feel safe, relaxed, and comfortable. Give them a few minutes to create that picture in their minds. Next, ask them to picture themselves in front of an audience and then ask them the following questions:

- What are you wearing?
- What time of day is it?
- What does the room look like?
- What kind of lighting do you have?
- How many people are there?
- What are you talking about?

Next ask them to visualize themselves at the end of their presentation. They have just delivered a flawless speech. The audience is smiling, standing, and clapping with enthusiasm. Give the participants a little time to "savor the moment." After they have had an opportunity to "experience" their taste of success, ask them to open their eyes and discuss with the person next to them how they felt. Most people will respond that they felt very good and enjoyed the feeling of success. The message here, of course, is for them to use this technique to help overcome stage fright every time they are asked to make a presentation or give a speech.

Another powerful technique trainers can use to reinforce their learning points is to tell stories -- stories from their own experience. Stories help the trainer relate to the group, and they help the participants identify with the trainer.

Not only does storytelling help create a high trust level between trainer and participants, stories help the message come alive. For example, in a "Presentation Skills" class, I have shared my story about going blank and completely forgetting my speech during a speech contest in high school. I tell the story to illustrate the danger of memorizing and over preparing. The story also illustrates the point that although it was an embarrassing and traumatic experience, I didn't let it stop me. Here I am many years later -- a professional speaker!

Bringing It to a Close

Endings are just as important as the rest of the training program. Remember: It's not what you give them, but what they take away that counts. There are many activities you can use to make your training unforgettable.

Remember the "What Do You Want to Know" activity where participants wrote their questions and expectations on Post-it notes?

To bring your training session full circle, ask the participants to get up and reclaim, or take off, their notes if their question or expectation was addressed. If you've done your job, then the flip chart pages on the wall will be empty. Not only does this activity bring closure to the session, it reinforces the learning. By reclaiming their questions, the participants have taken ownership and are acknowledging that their needs have been met.

Another effective closing technique is the human continuum. At the end of a training session, post two signs, one at each end of a long wall. For example, one sign might read "Competent" and the other, "Clueless." Ask the participants to envision the wall as a continuum. Ask them to think about where they were in terms of their knowledge of the subject and/or skill level at the beginning of the session. Then ask them to stand up and place themselves where they think they were on the continuum. Then ask a few participants to share why they placed themselves where they did. Next, ask them to think about where they are on the continuum at the end of the program and place themselves accordingly. Once again, ask participants to share the reasons for their placement. Most people will have moved from the "Clueless" end to the "Competent." Sometimes, however, the reverse happens. Those who come to the session thinking they "know it all" will often discover that they didn't know as much as they thought they did. Consequently, they will indicate a movement in the opposite direction.

In either case, this activity is a powerful way to help participants assess how much they perceive they have learned.

Like any other presentation, a successful training session is the result of careful planning, preparation and practice. Effective trainers use a skillful blend of content and participant interaction to create a program that not only involves and informs, but influences others to assimilate new information, modify attitudes, and change behaviors in both their professional and personal lives.

Karen Lawson, Ph.D., CSP, international speaker, author, and consultant, is president of Lawson Consulting Group in Lansdale, PA. She is the author or co-author of eight books, including The Art of Influencing *(Kendall/Hunt Publishing Company), and has published dozens of articles in professional journals. You can reach her at: 800-269-0797, www.LawsonCG.com.*

Touching Your Audience's Minds & Hearts with Stories

by Joanna Campbell Slan

In an age where people expect to be entertained, and click a button to change channels if they aren't, great speakers must be great storytellers or risk losing their audiences. Whether you are talking about attitude, teambuilding or total quality, spell-binding stories help you grab and hold people's attention.

Listen to people at any get-together, and you will hear stories. We think in stories, we talk in stories, and our lives form dynamic stories as each day unfolds. The stories told by professional speakers are no different than the stories you tell your friends over a cup of coffee with one exception: Professional speakers find, tell and remember stories deliberately not haphazardly.

Professional speakers use stories for a variety of reasons:

1. Stories illustrate major points. The best speakers support their main points by inviting their listeners to "step into" stories. In becoming the protagonist, the listener is transformed. Because we suffer no consequences by hearing stories, we can savor each moment and still take away valuable lessons. When the topic is controversial, a story may gently explore the more sensitive aspects of a situation. When the point is obscure, a story may hammer home the salient ideas.

2. Stories help us remember new ideas and information. A favorite history teacher of mine in high school made dead people come alive by telling us stories about American pioneers. People remember stories more than isolated information, because stories give information context. This allows the storyteller to share content in an engaging manner.

A speaker friend of mine once received this phone call from a meeting planner. "We're having this conference, and I simply had to call you," explained the meeting planner. "Jane Doe told me the story you told about the secretary who was having a problem. Gee, we all need to hear that story! It was so inspirational. Please send me the information; we need to book you."

Long after the speech was over, the story had a life of its own. In chemistry, they teach us that atoms have lives and half-lives, a quantifiable period it takes for the particle to die. Stories seem to take an opposite path. They live on and on, sometimes actually picking up energy and momentum. This helps explain why a book or movie goes from being a "sleeper" to a blockbuster.

3. Stories keep the audience engaged. In school, no matter how boring the teacher, you were forced to sit and listen. In real life, people get up and walk out. If you are lucky, they don't throw vegetables as they walk by.

People hire speakers for their stories. Good speakers work for years to craft messages so compelling that audiences lose all track of time. The finest speakers evoke laughter and tears from their listeners, aiding the group to share in a sort of emotional catharsis. Without using stories, it is difficult, if not impossible, to keep the audience interested in what you have to say. Stories keep your audiences entertained and hungry for more.

Human Drama

Human drama lays at the heart of all great stories. Classically, there are only three types of human drama: man against man; man against society; and man against God/nature. So, the movie "The Fugitive" is about man against society, because the protagonist is being tracked down by law enforcement officials (society). "Jaws" is a movie about man vs. nature, with nature taking the form of a shark. "The First Wives' Club" is a film about man against man, or to be more accurate, women vs. men.

At its core, human drama parallels the struggles -- small and large -- that each of us meet on a daily basis. We are not human beings struggling to be spiritual, but rather spiritual beings struggling to be human. In that struggle, we stumble, we fall and we get back up again. Because the struggle is the drama, all stories include some element of change which we also call action. Too often, speakers connect human drama with human tragedy and ignore the great, but less painful, everyday stories which tell us so much about the nature of being human. A flat tire, missing an airline flight, the hug of a child, are at once compelling, human, and ubiquitous. Thus, the small triumphs and tribulations of life should not be overlooked, since they represent the fabric of everyday life which we can all understand.

Looking at stories from this view of ordinary life, we see

that arguing with a co-worker qualifies as a man against man conflict, hitting a deer with the family car exemplifies man against nature, and sitting in a traffic jam serves to prove modern man's daily struggles against society.

Don't miss the best stories you can tell by waiting for high comedy or tragedy. Focus instead on the small drop of water that represents the vast ocean of life.

Where to Find Good Stories

The sages say, "That which is most personal is most universal." By sharing a slice of your life, you connect with your audience in powerful ways. Human beings hunger to know each other. We wonder, "Does anyone understand how I feel?" When we hear stories, we are reassured that the other person is not so different from us. This modern life, filled with alienation and isolation, seems infinitely more bearable when we are not alone.

Where can you find slice-of-life vignettes?

1. What do you tell your spouse, your children, or your friends about your day?

2. What was it like for you when you were growing up?

3. What did you overhear while waiting for the bus, train or airplane?

4. What did you see while buying groceries, picking up

your child from school, or walking to the mailbox?

5: What made you laugh, cry, smile or get angry as you moved through your day?

In the movie, "Defending Your Life," Albert Brooks' character dies and goes to a review station before he is sent to either heaven or eternal damnation. By conducting your own life review, you can revive stories that you can use from the platform. Start by creating a time line. It might look like this:

Date of birth
▼
First school days
▼
Junior high
▼
High school
▼
Upper education
▼
First job
▼
First romance
▼
Marriage
▼
Death of a parent
▼
First child
▼
First home
▼
Career

At each juncture, try to fill in a date and a story or two.

Memory Jogging Questions:

1. What is my earliest memory? What was my favorite toy?

2. Which teachers do I remember from grade school? Who was my favorite?
3. What was it like to move on to junior high? Was scared?
4. What interesting, significant events occurred to me while I was in high school?
5. How did I choose a college? What was my first roommate like?
6. When did I get my first job? What did it teach me? What was it?
7. Do I remember my first kiss? Who was it with? What was the setting?
8. What do I remember about my wedding? What was perfect? What went wrong?
9. Have I lost any parents or grandparents? How? What do I miss about that person?
10. What was it like to become a parent? What can I say about my children?
11. Do I remember my first adult home? The first house I bought? The house I brought my first child home to?
12. When did I discover the difference between a job and a career? What are my career high points and low points?

To assist you in your recollections, you may wish to use movies as memory joggers. If you want to remember high school, watch "American Graffiti" and "Peggy Sue Got Married." To recall the transition from high school to college, check out "The Four Friends" or "Breaking Away." To celebrate your wedding again, view "Four Weddings and a Funeral" or "Crossing Delancey." To relive the pain of losing an older relative, watch "On Golden Pond." Movies that celebrate the joy of parenthood include "She's Having a Baby" and "Parenthood." To reconnect with the value of having a career, you won't want to miss "Mr. Holland's Opus."

Each movie is not just one story, but a variety of stories woven together. Your life is a rich repository of stories, yours and those of each of your family members. Now might be the perfect time to capture your family memories, before you lose someone dear to you and all the wonderful stories that only that person can tell.

Structure of Stories

All stories have a beginning, a middle and an end. When we chat with a friend, we may muddy the three, crossing back and forth by saying, "Oh, and I forgot to tell you ... ." When you polish your story, systematically arrange the information to produce the biggest bang for your buck.

Start by dividing your story into its three parts. What is the beginning? The listener must have immediate information to locate your story in time and space. Give the listener the essential basics as quickly and concretely as possible: who, what, when, where and why. Now move to the middle. What action or actions propel your story along? Without action, nothing changes. Change must occur, or you don't have a story. Years ago, people amused themselves by creating dramatic tableaus.

They would create costumes and scenes which they would then unveil before a home audience to amuse the crowd. Today, we are hooked on action. This modern "drug" compels us to live restless lives seeking our next "hit." Action can be internal, as we think through a problem and develop possible solutions. Or, action can be external, as we move and the story moves with us.

Last of all, consider your ending. What is the climax? How is the situation resolved?

Significant Detail

As master speaker and storyteller Lou Heckler admonishes speakers, "Don't be the camera. Instead rob the bank." By skillful use of significant detail, you invite the listener to step into the story rather than to sit passively on the sidelines. Any concrete, sensory experience offers significant detail. Revisit your story. Ask yourself these questions:

1. What did the situation look like? What were the people involved wearing? Did they have any nervous habits? For example, you could say, "The office was a mess," or you could say, "The office looked like a copier vomited papers all over it." Which is more vivid? The first sentence asks you to believe me. The second paints a picture in your mind.

2. What did the story smell like? In the movie

"Michael," the angel smells like baked cookies, reinforcing the idea of life's fleeting homespun joy.

3. What did the story sound like? Humorist Steve Rizzo tells a fabulous story about an acting job he had doing voice-over work for a movie that was to be shown on television. Rizzo was to imitate Jack Nicholson, creating "clean" words and phrases so that the "blue" language in the movie could be replaced. As Rizzo walked around imitating Nicholson, his young son picked up the voice and the attitude. The result was a hilarious encounter with a waitress as young Rizzo looking quizzically at an oversized dessert spoon and saying à la Nicholson, "Gee, lady, did ya hafta bring me a darn shovel?"

4. What did the story "taste" like? Was there food involved? In every mystery featuring detective V.I. Warsharski, V.I. cooks Italian food for herself when she wants to be comforted. Author Sara Paretsky outlines the ingredients so precisely you could use the novel as a cookbook.

5. What did it feel like? In *At Paradise Gate*, Jane Smiley describes an interaction between mother and child: "Although Anna loved Claire's, and each child's, smiles and waves and kisses, loved too the stroke of a little hand on her breast while the child nursed, chancing upon this quiet business with a piece of cloth had touched her the most. It was so mysteriously inward when you hardly yet believed that the child had an

inner life." Smiley's writing, so sensual and specific, evokes instant recall to any woman who has ever nursed a child. The author captures two levels of feelings, the kinesthetic and the emotional.

Summary

By finding the stories inherent in your daily life; distinguishing their beginnings, middles and ends; and telling them in such a way to invite your listener to experience them, you will become a spell-binding storyteller.

As with any skill, storytelling grows with practice. Choose a few key stories and work with them. Then try them on everyone you meet. Don't give up easily. Work with the stories, or with a coach, and polish them to perfection.

If we could leave this world but one gift, a gift that touches hearts and unlocks closed minds would assure us that our lives were worthwhile. You can leave that gift by working on your skills as a master storyteller.

Joanna Campbell Slan is the author of Using Stories and Humor: Grab Your Audience, *a textbook for speechwriters and speechmakers. An award-winning speaker and presenter, you can contact Joanna at joannaslan@aol.com. To learn more about her work, including Joanna's line of inspirational books, books on scrapbooking, and her new mystery series which will debut in fall 2008, go to www.joannacampbellslan.com.*

SUGGESTED READINGS

The following books and other learning tools were either used in preparation for *Speaking Is An Audience-Centered Sport,* or are good resources for speakers.

Tom Antion,
Wake 'Em Up! Business Presentations
Anchor Publishing

Suzanne Bates
Speak Like a CEO
McGraw-Hill

Peter Urs Bender and Robert A. Tracz
Secrets of Face-to-Face Communication
The Achievement Group

Dianna Booher
Speak With Confidence
McGraw-Hill

Marjorie Brody, CSP, CMC, PCC, CPAE
"Effective Presentation Skills: Revitalize Your Speaking Style" (CD-ROM)
Career Skills Press

Joan Detz
How to Write and Give a Speech
St. Martin's Griffin

Ralph E. Himman, Ph.D
Dynamic Presentations: Using Your Voice and Body for Impact
Allyn & Bacon

James C. Humes
How to Become an Effective Speaker & Communicator
NewsMaxMedia

Timothy J. Koegel
The Exceptional Presenter
Greenleaf Book Group Press

Thomas Leech
How to Prepare, Stage & Deliver Winning Presentations
AMACOM

Michael MacFarlane
Share and Grow Rich: The Dottie Walters Effect
Elevate

Jim Meisenheimer
The 12 Best Questions to Ask Customers
Helbern Group

Jim Meisenheimer
50 More Ways to Sell Smarter
Helbern Group

Lilly Walters
Secrets of Superstar Speakers
McGraw-Hill

Roy Underhill
Khrushchev's Shoe: And Other Ways to Captivate an Audience of 1 to 1,000
Basic Books

ABOUT MARJORIE BRODY, CSP, PCC, CPAE SPEAKER HALL OF FAME
Speaker / Author / Executive Coach

Marjorie Brody, CSP, PCC, CPAE Speaker Hall of Fame, one of "Pennsylvania's 1999 Best 50 Women in Business," is the Founder and Fearless Leader of BRODY Professional Development. She acts in four distinct capacities: company president, professional speaker, executive coach and published author.

As an internationally recognized speaker, Marjorie proudly wears the designation of CSP -- Certified Speaking Professional, so designated by the National Speakers Association (NSA). In July 2006, she was inducted into NSA's Council of Peers Award for Excellence "Speaker Hall of Fame." Marjorie also earned her PCC – Professional Certified Coach -- designation from the International Coach Federation; and the title of CMC – Certified Management Consultant – from the Institute of Management Consultants. She is the only professional worldwide to obtain the combined CSP, CMC and PCC titles.

In October 2006, Marjorie was inducted into the Temple University "Women's Entrepreneurial Hall of Fame." She was one of 12 women selected as "1999 Distinguished National Leaders" by the National Association of Women Business Owners, Greater Philadelphia Chapter. She was also one of 25 women selected as "1999 Women of

Distinction" by the *Philadelphia Business Journal,*
National Association of Women Business Owners and
The Forum of Executive Women. Marjorie's company,
BRODY, was a finalist in the small business category for
the "2001 Family Business of the Year Award," coordinated by Wharton Small Business Development Center.
Marjorie was also a finalist in the Ernst & Young 2002
and 2001 "Entrepreneur of the Year" awards, in the business consulting category.

Her topics include business etiquette, presentation skills,
turning business and career dreams into reality, and effective self-marketing. Marjorie travels extensively as a professional speaker and executive coach, sharing her knowledge with people in the U.S. and abroad. Through repeat
business and referrals, she has built up an impressive
client roster of *Fortune* 100 and 500 companies.

A well-published writer and author, Marjorie Brody has
authored more than 18 books, including *Career MAGIC:
A Woman's Guide to Reward & Recognition, Speaking Is An
Audience-Centered Sport, Professional Impressions ...
Etiquette for Everyone, Every Day,* and the award-winning
Help! Was That a Career Limiting Move? Marjorie is pro-
filed on several speaking- and training-related sites on the
Web, and has two home pages: www.BrodyPro.com and
www.MarjorieBrody.com.

Members of the national media regularly contact
Marjorie for her commentary on a variety of workplace
and career issues – including CNBC, Fox-TV, Oxygen,

ABCNews.com, CNN.com, *The Wall Street Journal, USA Today, The Washington Post, People, Fortune* and *BusinessWeek*. She has contributed career/etiquette columns for *BusinessWeek* online, and other sites.

Marjorie is a Professor Emeritus at Bucks County Community College, a past president of National Speakers Association, Mid-Atlantic Chapter (NSAMAC), a member of the National Speakers Association (where she is also a National Board Director), Institute of Management Consultants, the American Society for Training and Development, International Coach Federation, The Forum of Executive Women, a founding member of Master Speakers International and Business Builders, and a founding professor of Mentor U.com. She is also a member of the editorial advisory board for *communication briefings* newsletter. Marjorie was NSAMAC "Chapter Member of the Year" in 1997 and NSAMAC's "Speaker of the Year" in 1999. Her company, BRODY Professional Development, has WBE certification – Women's Business Enterprise.

INDEX

A

Acceptance speech, 183-184
Antion, Tom, 221-228
Audience members, 7-12
    apathetic, 31-32
    getting their attention, 68-70
    demographics, 9-10
    favorable, 30
    hostile, 30-31
    interacting, 263-265
    involvement, 73-74, 262-263
    profile, 9
    psychographics, 11-12
    types of, 30-33

B

Body of presentation, 70-76
    sample, 79
    supporting materials, 72-73
Body language, 119
    examples, 120-121
Boyd, Ty, 228-232
Breathing, 102-104

C

Call to action (persuasion), 29-30
Campbell Slan, Joanna, 270-280
Cause and effect (informative speech), 24

Charts, 57
       design tips, 61
       sample, 60
Chronological order (informative speech), 22-23
       example of, 22
Competence, 27-28
Conclusion, 75-76
       sample, 80
Connor, Tim, 253-260
Conviction, 27-28
Convince (persuasion), 29
Creating persuasive presentations, 26-27
Credibility, 27-28

D
Decision makers, 11-12
Delivery
       dynamics, 105
       five styles of, 94
       how to perfect, 141-143
       techniques, 87-90
Demographics, 9-10
Diction, 131
Drafts, 80-81
Dress, 105-114

E
Emotional connection with audience, 74
Emphasis, 131-132
Entertaining speech, 7
Ethos, 26-28

Eulogies, 185
Examples (use of), 67, 71
Expromptu style, 91, 94
Extemporaneous style, 90-91, 94
Eye contact, 117-118

F

Facial expressions, 118
Facts (use of), 15-16, 67
Flip charts, 51, 54
Farewell speech, 187-188
Favorable audience, 30

G

Geographical order (of informative speech), 23
Gestures, 119-129
    effective, 125-128
    what not to do, 120-124
    what to do, 125-129
Graphs, 56-59
    bar, 56, 58
    circle, 56-57
    line, 56, 59
    pictographs, 56, 59
    profile, 56, 58
Grooming, 115, 168

H

Handouts, 54-55
Hillman, Ralph E., 232-246

Hostile audience, 30-31
Hostility, 147-148
Humor, 17-19, 67-68, 100, 221-228

I

Illustration (use of), 67
Impromptu style, 87-90
Inauguration speech, 184-185
Informative speech, 5-6
    organization of, 22-24
Informative presentation planning sheet, 25
Information (collecting and using), 14-16
International presentations, 205-212
Internet meetings, 171-179
Interpreters, 208-209
Introduction, 65-70, 78-79
    sample, 78-79
    speeches of, 183

K

Know (must, should, could), 74-75

L

Language (vulgar), 19
Lawson, Karen, 260-270
Learning styles, 11
Line drawings, 57
Logistics, 13-14, 33-34
Logos, 26

M

Manuscript style, 91-92, 94
Master of ceremonies, 185-186, 228-232
Meetings, 157-179
    closing, 165-166
    evaluating, 164-165
    leader of, 155-156
    moderator, 156-157
    planning worksheet, 160
    sample agenda, 161
Memorized style, 92-93
Mixed audience, 32-33
    favorable mix, 32
    hostile mix, 32-33
Moderator, 156-157
Motivated sequence, 37-39, 44
Motivation (persuasion), 29
Movement, 116-117
Multimedia presentations, 49-51

O

Online demonstrations, 189-198
Online presenting, 171-179
Organizing
    your presentation, 20-22
    persuasive presentation, 34-36, 39
Orientation (new employee), 186-187
Outline
    developing, 21-22
    sample, 78-80

P

PAL™, 4, 7, 21, 77
Past-Present-Future (informative speech), 24
Pathos, 26-27
Pauses, 132-133
Pelletier, Ray, 249-253
Pepe, Michele, 189-197, 205-212
Persuasive speaking, models of 44-45
Persuasive speech, 6
Persuasive presentations
    creating, 26
    purpose of, 28-30
    organizing, 34-45
    planning sheets, 36, 39, 43
Phrase outline method, 21-22
Point of view, 72-73
Posture, 115-118
    and movement, 116-117
PowerPoint, 50, 62-63, 171-172
Power robbers, 135-138
Practice, 82-86, 143
PREP model, 89-91
Presentations
    organizing, 20-24
    skills for trainers, 260-270
    special occasions, 180-188
    special types, 152-179
    three main parts, 67-79
Preparation process, 4-5
Preview your subject, 69-70
Proposition to proof, 34-36, 44

Psychographics (audience), 11-12
Purpose, 5-7

Q
Questions, 66
    control, 147-148
    encourage, 145-146
    hostility (how to handle), 147-148
    respond to, 148-150
    tag, 138-139
    VIPP technique, 147-148
Questions and answers 144-151
Quotations, 17, 67, 71

R
Radde, Paul O., 246-248
Remey Pepe, Michele, 189-198, 205-212
Reflective, 40-45

S
Seating (audience), 246-248
Self-talk, 98-99
Selling, 253-260
Slan, Joanna Campbell, 270-280
Software, 189-198
Spatial order
    of informative speech, 23
    example of, 23
Speaking
    to lead and inspire, 217-221

persuasive, 34-45

special occasions, 180-188

Speech, 5

types of, 5-7

organization, 22-24, 77-78

Speechwriters, 213-217

Stage fright, 95-104

control, 100-101

helpful breathing techniques & exercises, 101-103

managing physical symptoms, 103-104

Statistics (use of), 15-17, 71-74

Steele, William R., 198-205, 217-221

Stewart, Bob, 213-217

Stories, 15-17, 67, 71, 270-280

T

Talk (fast/slow), 130-131

Team leader, 155-156

Team presentations, 153-156

Technical material (how to present), 198-205

Three Ts (touch, turn and talk), 54

Timing tip (for practice), 84-85

Toastmaster (master of ceremonies), 185-186

Topical order (of informative speech), 24

Trainers

presentation skills for, 260-270

Transitions (use of), 72

sample, 79-80

Trustworthiness, 27-28

U
Uninformed audience, 32

V
Verbal, 134-141, 207-208
Videoconferences, 166-170
Visual, 105-129, 139-140
Video systems, 48-49
VIPP, 147-148
Visualization, 16, 37-38, 99
Visual aids, 16-17, 22, 46-64, 71
       choosing, 47-48
       constructing, 55-56
       practice with, 83
       rules for use, 62-64
       types of, 48-51, 54-57
       what not to do, 52
       what to do, 53
Vocal, 129-132, 140, 206-207
Voice
       problems, 133-134
       training, 232-248
Volume, 130
Vulgar language, 19

W
Wardrobe, 106-116, 172
       business casual, 108-109, 111-113
       business professional, 107-111
       classic casual, 111
       dress down/weekend wear, 114

　　　resort casual, 113
　　　smart casual, 112
　　　men, 107-108
　　　women, 108-109
Web conferences, 171-179
Webinars, 171-179
Welcome speech, 182
WIIFM (what's in it for me?), 12, 70-71, 134
WIIFT (what's in it for them?), 68, 77